"Tony is a longtime friend who has impeccable integrity and immeasurable wit. Tony Ingle is to basketball and life as E. F. Hutton was to the financial market. When Tony talks, people listen! Tony's life experiences in this book will be enjoyable to all readers. Sit back and relax, you'll be thoroughly entertained! "

BOB REINHART, FORMER HEAD COACH, GEORGIA STATE UNIVERSITY / NBA SCOUT

"I laughed and cried reading this heartwarming and inspirational book. If you combined the movies Rudy, Hoosiers and Miracle On Ice, I beleive this story tops them all. Coach Tony's against-all-odds story to become a National Champion is amazing!"

JASON HEWLETT, ENTERTAINER / SPEAKER/AUTHOR

"Every once in a while the world gives birth to a true original. When that happens it behooves the world to capture the essence of that true original like lightning in a bottle. Tony's story will make you laugh and cry, often at the same time.

Above all else, Tony's story will make you marvel at the depth of the human spirit found inside this impoverished boy born into an impoverished home and time. Tony and his family's triumph over unrelenting adversity persuades us that a portion of that same human spirit lies inside each and every one of us, that we are our own bit of lightning in a bottle."

MITCH DAVIS, FILMMAKER

D0109083

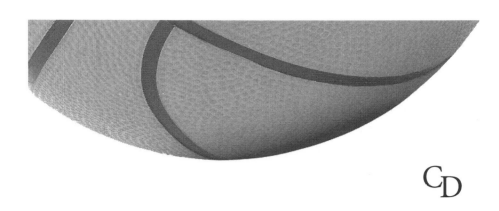

CD

I DON'T MIND
HITTING BOTTOM,
I JUST HATE DRAGGING
TONY INGLE with KYLE WHELLISTON

Photographs courtesy of the author. Used by permission.

Printed in the United States of America
First printing: November 2009
Second printing: January 2012
Third printing: November 2014
Fourth printing: November 2018

LIBRARY OF CONGRESS CATALOGING-IN-PUBLICATION DATA
Ingle, Tony.
I I Don't Mind Hitting Bottom, I Just Hate Dragging / Tony Ingle with Kyle
Whelliston. p. cm.

ISBN 978-0-615-32931-4

1. Basketball. 2. Ingle, Tony - Biography. I. Title. 3. Whelliston, Kyle.

Book design by Roni Lagin and Kyle Whelliston

"Tony is one of the nicest and most sincere men I've ever met. He is a great role model, and he inspires me to be a better person daily... He will inspire you with his story."

BILL SELF, HEAD COACH, UNIVERSITY OF KANSAS

"I have known Tony for many years, and he is a great person and a great coach. He has an incredible story to tell and I have always admired his faith."

BILLY DONOVAN, HEAD COACH, UNIVERSITY OF FLORIDA

"I've known Tony for a long time. He's a great example for all of us. Adversity happens, and how you handle it is the key. Tony just keeps punching."

DOC RIVERS, HEAD COACH, BOSTON CELTICS

"Coach Tony Ingle is one of those rare coaches who realize that coaching is more than teaching basketball... it's about helping young people realize their potential and more importantly keep meaningful relationships along the way. I'm honored to know him and his family."

SHAWN BRADLEY, FORMER BYU AND NBA PLAYER

"The thing I admire most about Tony Ingle is that he kept the faith and pursued his dream. This book is a classic example of having a goal and following a daily plan to achieve it."

THAD MATTA, HEAD COACH, OHIO STATE UNIVERSITY

"A man who has known hardships throughout his life. A walking, talking made-for-TV movie."

DOUG ROBINSON, DESERET NEWS

"I have known Tony Ingle for over 30 years. I first knew him as a great high school coach and I watched him make the transition to college. Seeing him win a national championship was no great surprise because I knew he had it in him. He loves the game of basketball and is one of the most enthusiastic coaches in the game today. Tony is successful because of his great enthusiasm and determination. I'm proud to have him as a good friend."

BOBBY CREMINS, HEAD COACH, COLLEGE OF CHARLESTON

"Don't call it a comeback... if you want to measure success, Tony Ingle stands alone as someone who has risen through all the elements of life... and has earned the success and gratitude of his peers."

MARTY BLAKE, DIRECTOR OF NBA SCOUTING SERVICES

"Tony Ingle is a great story teller, but the real story is how he has been able to overcome adversity, physical and health issues, as well as failure... and turn that into championships on a national scale. A great family man whose whole family has given back to basketball together. This will be a great read! "

SONNY SMITH, FORMER HEAD COACH, AUBURN UNIVERSITY

FOR MY FAMILY

THOSE THAT HAVE PASSED

THOSE WHO ARE LIVING

THOSE TO COME

CONTENTS

FOREWORDS

TONY INGLE HAS ONE OF THE MOST COMPELLING AND inspirational stories in all of basketball. He has faced adversity head on, overcome obstacles that got in his way, and accepted professional challenges that most people would frown upon. He is a proven winner who has been successful at every step of his journey, striving to become an NCAA Division I head coach.

He has worked hard to reach his full potential as a coach. He has done it the right way and his way – by making it entertaining for the fans, enlightening for the media, educational for his players, and rewarding for those who hired him.

I first met Tony when I was coaching for the Atlanta Hawks. We invited him to work our camps. I immediately found out some interesting things about Tony. For one, we sent him after morning coffee for 15 coaches. When he returned, he had only four cups of coffee. Now try to explain that to 15 pro and college coaches. Later, after camp, I invited the staff out for a beer. When I placed the order, I felt a tap on my shoulder. When I turned around, there was Tony asking me if I could be so kind to change his order from cold beer to soda pop. I later found out that Tony doesn't drink coffee or beer.

The next day at camp, some members of our staff were sharing Tony Ingle stories. One story involved him getting his players to turn cartwheels in the middle of games.

Another story: Tony's Cherokee High School team was playing Marietta High School (which just so happened to have 6-foot-9 future NBA standout Dale Ellis on its roster). Tony came up with a trick play called the "shake and bake." Now, get this picture in your mind: it's a big game, the place is packed, and his team is down five points with the ball out of bounds underneath the basket. Tony called time out to encourage and reinforce instructions. The players returned to the court and got into their respective positions.

Then, on the slap of the ball, three of Tony's players dropped to the floor – jerking, shaking, and pretending to have seizures. A Marietta player bent over to assist a player who was convulsing on the floor, and the ball was tossed to the front of the rim where a CHS player scored on a layup! The place went nuts! The crowd was hysterical!

This is a true story.

This camp was my first association with this "Ingle guy," and I was absolutely convinced that he was completely and literally off-the-wall. I knew that as the owner of the camp, I had to keep a close eye on him.

And for the next 30 years, I did just that. I kept a close eye on him... and found a devout family man, workaholic, teacher, and a courageous coach. Tony has the right ingredients for leadership, and he is always striving for excellence.

Plus, he has one of the greatest comeback stories in sports history. Tony took over as the interim head coach at BYU and finished with a record of 0-19. He was out of coaching for three years. He lost his job, his house, but never his dream.

Let me ask you: would you hire a coach who went 0-19?

Well, this is where his story becomes incredible. Not only did he get a head coaching job at Division II Kennesaw State University... but four years later, there was Tony Ingle standing in front of a national CBS-TV audience celebrating with his 2004 National Championship team.

I suggest you keep an eye on Tony as well. After a four-year mandated NCAA reclassifying period to move from Division II to Division I, Tony Ingle stands at the threshold of his dream of becoming a Division I head coach, and climbing another mountain all the way to the top.

HUBIE BROWN
TWO-TIME NBA HEAD COACH OF THE YEAR
BASKETBALL HALL OF FAME, CLASS OF 2005

— — — — — —

WHEN I RECEIVED THE REQUEST FROM TONY TO WRITE a foreword for this book, it didn't take me long to accept his offer. I believe in Tony and I know that his heart is in the right place for helping others.

I have known Tony and his family for years. We first met when he served as an assistant basketball coach at BYU. We also had an association when our children competed against each other in local sports programs. However, I really got to know him when he was hired as the interim head coach at BYU and was placed in an impossible situation.

It has been said that you can find out more about a man when things are going badly than when things are going well. This certainly holds true for Tony. The head coach at BYU was dismissed, and Tony was offered the interim head coaching job, to coach a floundering team with a 1-6 record. Tony accepted the challenge and finished that season with a 0-19 record and was branded as a coach that couldn't win a game.

He knew it would be hard for someone to hire him with that record. Tony and his family went through some extremely difficult financial and emotional times, including having the bank foreclose on their house. What was remarkable about Tony during this tough time was he had a strong emotional bank account and took the high road, not blaming others for his misfortunes. He was out of his chosen profession of coaching for three years.

My good friend Denis Waitley says, "When we are without, we should look within," and Tony did just that. He knew he had to stay active and avoid being caught up in self-pity.

During this time, he sold carpet and golf equipment, was an NBA scout for the Utah Jazz, became the founder and director of the John & Nellie Wooden Awards, and was a color commentator for Mountain West Conference games. He also joined the National Speakers Association where he could get back into coaching - only this time, it was from a podium.

The point I want to make is Tony had plenty of reasons to quit, to just give up and feel sorry for himself, but instead he was proactive and determined to get better. His dream (begin with the end in mind) never died. That's obvious by the way he continued to stay the course of self improvement, investing back into his pursuit of being an NCAA Division I head coach.

He got closer when he accepted a head coaching job at an NCAA Division II school in Georgia, Kennesaw State University. Amazingly, only four years after being hired, Coach Tony Ingle's team won the *National Championship,* live on CBS-TV!

The university applied for NCAA Division I status, and after a mandated reclassifying period set by the NCAA of 4 years, in the 2009-2010 season, Coach Ingle's team will be a full counter, with a chance to one day go to the NCAA Tournament and participate in March Madness as a NCAA Division I head coach.

Now, that is bouncing back!

I'm convinced that when you read *I Don't Mind Hitting Bottom, I Just Hate Dragging,* you will find a fun book that will add a little spice to your life. It'll be something you can relate to that will help you face adversity, overcome obstacles and accept professional challenges as well.

Through my associations with Tony Ingle, I have known him as both a coach and a professional speaker. I firmly believe, first and foremost, that what has helped him in both categories is that he sincerely cares about and loves people. He is real and authentic and has the unique ability to sense other people's pains and needs. Whether he is on the court or on stage, you will find wit and wisdom, and you will without a doubt be enlightened as well as entertained.

Tony leads by example, coaches with enthusiasm, and influences with the right touch of humility that we all enjoy and can relate to.

DR. STEPHEN R. COVEY
AUTHOR, "THE 7 HABITS OF HIGHLY EFFECTIVE PEOPLE" AND "THE 8TH HABIT"
PROFESSIONAL SPEAKER AND MANAGEMENT EXPERT

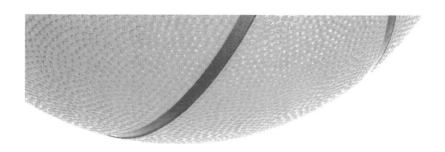

PROLOGUE

A LOT OF BOOKS ABOUT SPORTS START OUT BY TRYING to grab the reader's attention right off the bat. The author might lay out the scenario right before a big game, with the players preparing to go out and give their best. You're in the locker room, listening to the coach give the big pregame pep talk. Or page one might put you right in the middle of the action, with the clock winding down. Just seconds to go. There's tension in the air, the intensity so thick you can cut it with a knife!

Not my book.

This begins in the middle of January 1997, when I was the interim head coach at Brigham Young University. We were playing at Texas Christian on national television, and we were getting beat by 40 points. A slew of season-ending injuries had whittled our team down to eight freshmen and three walk-ons from the football team. And what's more, we had to compete in the Western Athletic Conference, which at the time was full of NCAA Tournament teams and future NBA stars. BYU was in the middle of a grueling schedule that had us playing 14 nationally ranked teams in 19 games.

The Horned Frogs were coached at the time by Billy Tubbs. I'll leave it to my friend Pat Bryson to describe Coach Tubbs: "He's the kind of guy you'd love to see in a bear hug... with a bear that hasn't been fed in two weeks."

Coach Tubbs' game plan has always been to overwhelm his opponents with explosive physical play. He likes to recruit long-armed sinewy athletes, and he runs those players through a brutal conditioning regimen to prepare them to dominate games by sheer force.

Billy tells you up front: "We're going to beat you. If you can't keep up with us, that's your fault."

That night, as an ESPN audience watched, TCU pressed and trapped BYU for 40 straight minutes. They beat the hell out of us. Up by 30 points, he left four of his five starters in the game, and never told them to ease up on us or show mercy. We had four freshmen on the court who were trying the best they could to compete, and they were attempting to salvage as much school spirit as they could before the game was over.

I have a rule when I coach. If my team's getting beat, I never sit down. I've seen a lot of coaches who will simply take a seat and sulk in these particular kinds of situations. Over my dead body, I say. If the crowd knows the game's over, and the announcers know everything's decided except for the final score, I am *not* going to sit down while my players are out there busting their butts on the floor.

Late in the game, I subbed in Nick Taggart, a big, awkward freshman forward who never got any playing time. As soon as he got in the game, he threw the ball into the crowd. I shouted a few words of encouragement and clapped my hands. The crowd let me have it. *"Sit down, Coach! Game's over, Coach!"* The final score was TCU 101, BYU 61.

I had accepted the interim position just a month earlier. Roger Reid had been the head coach at BYU for over seven years, and an assistant there for the previous 11. He was fired after opening the 1996-97 season with a dismal 1-6 record. I had been Coach Reid's top assistant since he'd been promoted, and we won a lot of games together – 157 of them, in fact. BYU went to five NCAA Tournaments during that time, and Roger was named WAC Coach of the Year twice.

But the run came to a crashing halt with a .500 season in 1995-96, and 1996-97 was off to a horrendous start. While on a December recruiting trip, I received a phone call from Rondo Fehlberg, the new athletic director at BYU.

"Tony, we have a mess on our hands," he said. "Compounding the problem is that we are *really* pressed for time. I'm not at liberty to discuss this in depth with you, but I'm calling to inform you that we have just dismissed Roger as head coach. We need somebody to coach the team for the remainder of the year."

He offered me the reins of the team, and the promise of serious consideration for the permanent job at the end of the season.

At first, I politely refused. It was professional suicide, I told Rondo. The injuries and the bad luck decimated our team. We weren't only losing, we were losing badly.

Washington beat us 95-44. Cal State Fullerton and Pacific, two midmajor programs we had scheduled to pad our record with easy wins, ended up ripping us apart. BYU hadn't entered league play yet, and I knew how good the WAC was going to be. Everybody did.

But the more I thought about it, the more I knew that I couldn't quit on our team. I had to stand up and support our players.

"I'll do it on one condition," I told Rondo. "I'll do it if you will not judge me on my win-loss record. If you judge me on how many wins I get, that's totally unfair."

He agreed, and I took on the role of BYU's interim head coach. I became the captain of the LZ 129 Hindenberg.

At first, the media and fans were hopeful that things would improve at BYU under my leadership. "Tony Ball," they called it. They were pumping me up as if I was the savior of the program or something.

But the problem was, Tony Ball didn't win a single game. I was 0-19 as the interim head coach at BYU.

We battled and scrapped every game, but what we didn't do was win ballgames. In a year when our conference sent eight teams to the national postseason, we became the WAC's punching bag - a scrimmage squad that teams like Utah and TCU and Tulsa used to tune up for each other. In early February, we lost at New Mexico by a 74-32 score. There was a six week period during which we lost every single game by double digits. We finished the season on a 21-game losing streak.

Through it all, my players never quit on me, because I didn't quit on them. Not a single one of those 1996-97 Cougars called out the coach in public, pointed fingers, or walked off the team. I had the support of the BYU booster club, most of the media, and a majority of the community. They all knew how difficult the situation was. Our last home game drew 13,000 fans, and an independent poll conducted at the end of the season found that I was the public's choice to receive the permanent head coaching job.

But there were some at BYU who didn't agree. Ten days after the season was over, I found myself in the office meeting with members of the university administration.

"We're having a press conference in the morning, and you're not our coach," the university president told me.

"The agreement was that you weren't supposed to judge me on my win-loss record," I protested.

"We didn't," the president explained. "We used you as a benchmark to hire another coach."

It was the most humiliating day of my life. I felt angry and betrayed, as if I was set up for failure from the start. I was the latest victim of a profession that demands perfection now and improvement later.

But as I left that meeting, I left them a little something to remember me by.

"Gentlemen," I said as I walked out the door. "If you ever want to win it all, give me a call."

It was one of those closing lines that must have sounded silly or crazy, especially from a coach that had just gone 0-19. But I meant every word.

I knew in my heart that I had a national championship in me, and not just one. I had worked my entire career to fulfill a promise I'd made to myself and my family many years beforehand. I had a dream to win a national title as a coach to make up for a self-perceived failure as a player. At BYU, I'd simply put my ladder against the wrong house.

My drive to get to the top without sacrificing my ideals and principles has defined the path my life has taken. Throughout the journey, I have carried with me my faith in God, my belief in myself, a spirit to serve, and courage to continue. I have not allowed rejection, adversity, momentary failure or abject poverty to stand between me and my goals. My reasons for persevering require an explanation of my character.

Which, I guess, requires starting at the very beginning.

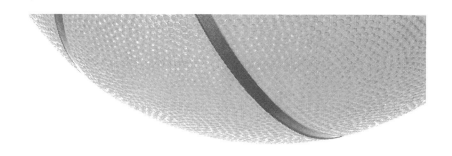

1
SMILING THROUGH THE PAIN

I WAS BORN WITH A FACE DEFORMITY, A FATTY TUMOR IN my jaw. When I was an infant, the tumor was growing so rapidly that it spread throughout my face. It caused severe damage to my facial muscles and nerves, my cheekbone, as well as my eyebrows and nose. The growth distorted my lips, and I began losing vision in my left eye.

I was always in and out of hospitals and doctor's offices. Erlanger Hospital in Chattanooga, Tennessee is where I spent a majority of my childhood.

My first memory: I was three years old, lying in a hospital bed, and I clearly recall that my mother was in my room. She was wearing a light blue shirt, asleep with arms folded, while I was recovering from a face operation. That is the very first memory I have of this life, and it was a memory of love. I felt such comfort, knowing that she was there with me.

My mother was guarding me from fear and loneliness.

Dr. Barnwell was my physician. He performed a face operation on me when I was three years old, and more at five, seven, eleven and also at thirteen. It was definitely not fun, going through operation after operation, which left my face full of scars and distorted.

When I was 10 years old and in the fifth grade, I missed two months of school because of some complications that arose after one of my operations. I had close to 2,000 stitches in my face. I was wrapped up like a mummy, with a shaved head and gauze bandages. It felt like I was living in a scuba helmet. There were two holes for my ears, one for my right eye, and one for my right nostril. There was another for my mouth – just big enough to fit a straw into.

I was never a good student in school. That was mostly because I missed so much time because of my operations. Once, I came home with a report card from Pleasant Grove Elementary School with five F's and one D. My dad called me over after he'd read it, and he told me, "Son, you're spending too much time on one subject."

As a result of all the classes I missed after my fifth grade face operation, Pleasant Grove held me back from advancing to the sixth grade. I often tell people that the best two years of my life were the fifth grade!

The operation that turned out to be my final surgery came when I was 13, and it consisted of sawing and grinding my cheekbone down. Three years later, I was scheduled to have plastic surgery, and I was so relieved that I was finally going to be normal.

But Dr. Barnwell was tragically killed by a drunken driver six months before my surgery date, and I was so shocked when my mother told me the horrible news one December day. I couldn't believe that God would allow such a smart and gifted man to die like that.

After months of awkward silence, I finally worked up the courage to ask my mother if I was still going to have my face fixed.

"Tony, there's something you need to know," she said. "Dr. Barnwell never charged us for any of your operations. One time, your daddy and I forced him to take $100. Now that he's passed on, we just can't afford to go through with it."

So you could say that I have a $100 face.

Trust me, I've heard my share of jokes about how I look. I received my share of name-calling as a child, and I was certainly made fun of a lot as I was growing up. I continue to hear comments through my adult life as well.

Nowadays, people say I have a pretty transparent personality; with me, what you see is definitely what you get. I've been described as an interesting person, as well as a lot of other adjectives I probably shouldn't mention here in this book. But it took me a very, very long time to develop a sense of humor about my particular condition.

We've all made fun of others when we were kids, and most of us have been made fun of at some point. But being the constant butt of jokes can really get old fast, especially when you're struggling to have a healthy self-esteem. I never got the opportunity to build any real self-confidence, because people were always telling me I'd never be married or that no girls would ever want to date me. Some kids were so cruel that they twisted and contorted their facial muscles to do Tony Ingle impressions.

It took me many years to learn that we all have some type of scars. Some people have scars on their bodies that can be covered up by clothing. Many hide emotional scars from the hurts of the past. Some even have financial scars that cannot be detected until years later.

When I was a child, I asked God, "Why me? Why should my scars be on my face? Why can't I hide them, even from myself?"

I couldn't hide my scars, because I couldn't hide my face.

Once, during my second year of fifth grade, I had enough. When Mr. Wiggins' number 35 bus pulled up at our home after school, I saw that my mother had arrived home from work early. I ran straight to the house, into the kitchen where my mom was standing washing the dishes.

"I hate my face! I hate school!" I screamed. "I hate being stupid, I hate being ugly, and I'm going to be this way all my life. I'm not ever going back. *Never!*"

I went up to my bedroom, and I lay there in bed crying my eyes out. I was feeling sorry for myself, having a major pity party.

Mother came in, and she sat on the side of the bed. She gently placed her hand on me as I continued to cry.

"Tony," she said. "I'm sorry you feel that way."

"You don't know what it's like to be ugly," I blurted out, tears soaking my pillow. "You don't know what it's like to have a crooked smile, with people making fun of you all the time. I wish I could just wear a mask to school, or even cut my head off. I wish I could hide my face... but I can't hide my ugly face!"

She lovingly and tenderly placed her arms around me, and pulled me close. With a mother's wisdom, she replied, "Son, you don't need to wear a mask. All you need to wear is a smile. Everybody has a smile, if they choose to use it."

"But all smiles aren't pretty or nice," I said. "I've got a crooked smile. Just look at my ugly mouth."

"Oh no, that's not true," she said. "Every smile is beautiful, regardless of the shape of the teeth or the angle of the lips. So what if your smile is crooked? It is much better to smile with a crooked mouth than to have perfectly shaped lips and never smile at all. Tony, please never stop smiling. Others might try to cause you pain because of the way you look, but you must remember to always smile."

Her point was well-taken, and her words sank deep into my heart and mind. I decided then, as a young boy, that I would wear a smile on my face instead of hiding behind a mask. My mother made me realize that I had nothing to be ashamed of. I might never be normal, but I could make the decision to smile through the pain.

So I've been wearing a smile ever since. Even though I'll never be in a toothpaste commercial, I use my smile more often than most people. I also love to see other people smile. Smiling is the true universal language; it means the same thing in every culture on earth. When you feel good, and have a smile on your face, you perform better. When you smile at someone, more often than not they'll smile back. Wouldn't it be a better world if everyone smiled more?

Later that school year, a photographer came to take class pictures. All of us kids were waiting our turn to sit in front of the camera. When I sat down in the chair, the photographer took one look at me and asked very solemnly, "Son, will you turn to the good side?" A hush came over everyone in line.

"Yes, sir, I will," I replied. "If you tell me which one it is. Which side do you want me to turn to?"

One time, when I was a teenager, I was purchasing something at the grocery store. There was a lady behind the counter, a big fat lady, she looked like she somehow got her mouth stuck on an air hose. She was about four-foot-eleven and weighed about 411 pounds. Honestly, I didn't know if she walked or rolled to work. I walked up to the counter.

"What in the world happened to your face?" she asked, completely shocked.

"I don't know," I replied. "I didn't ask you how much you weighed." The guy in back of me in the checkout line just about died laughing.

— — — — — —

During my childhood, the only thing that kept me sane was basketball. I loved to play, so I went out for the team at Pleasant Grove. Two fifth graders made the squad, me and Joey Bryant. We didn't get jerseys, though. Joey got a t-shirt, and I got one too. So my very first basketball uniform consisted of a t-shirt with number zero on the back, and a pair of silky maroon shorts with gold stripes on the sides.

I remember the very first time I got to play in an organized basketball game. We were beating Varnell; I think the score was something like 56-4. The coach must have felt like it was safe to put me in, so I got to play for a few minutes. I was dribbling up the floor, I got to about halfcourt and he said, "Shoot!"

What he meant was that I was to dribble up the floor, and to take a shot whenever I found a clear opportunity. But I was so nervous, I wanted to make sure I did exactly what my coach told me to. So I grabbed hold of the ball at half-court, and I just *let it fly*. The first shot I ever took was from 47 feet out.

And I banked it in!

Another time, we were playing Cohutta, and it was a close game in the late stages – tied at 55 with less than a minute to go. Coach had to put me in because one of the starters had fouled out, and as soon as a teammate passed me the ball, a Cohutta player hacked me.

"Hey," my coach yelled out at the referee. "He didn't foul Ingle, he fouled somebody else!"

Coach was trying to pull a fast one, but I was too dumb to understand what was going on. "No, Coach, he fouled *me*."

"Shut up," my coach called out to me. "Don't you want to win?" I got to the foul line, and my first shot went right over the backboard. I was scared to death. My next shot hit the net. Well, the outside of it, anyway. I went home and bawled my eyes out because I felt like I had let my teammates down. I had cost us the game.

But as far as I can remember, I never again missed a free throw with the game on the line. Ever.

In the spring of my eighth grade year, word got around Pleasant Grove that nearby North Whitfield High School had a new coach coming in. His name was Brady Creel. He decided to hold spring tryouts, because he wanted to see what kind of talent was coming in for his first year on the job.

I asked my dad if he could buy me some shoes, so I could go out for the team. He cussed me out and told me that I wasn't going to spend my high school years playing games and wasting my time. Then I asked my mother, something I didn't want to do, and I ended up bothering her so much that she scraped together enough money to go down to Cox's One Stop Shop.

When she came home with that shoebox, I was hysterical with joy. But when I opened the box and saw those shoes, I saw that they were slip-ons with elastic on the sides. They looked like deck shoes straight out of an episode of "Gilligan's Island". I knew she meant well, and I didn't want to break her heart by expressing my disappointment.

But I could definitely not play basketball in those shoes.

I remember going home every day that week, climbing up on the kitchen counter. There I'd sit in the sink, staring out the kitchen window. I watched all my friends from Pleasant Grove walking to the gym for tryouts. But all I could do is just sit there and imagine. It was the loneliest feeling in the world.

— — — — — —

Our family was poor by anybody's standards. We had so little money that we met the criteria to live in the government housing projects of Dalton, Georgia – a city an hour north of Atlanta that's known as the "carpet capital of the world."

Our small house had brick and cinder-block walls, and the floors were made of painted concrete. The manager would deliver a few buckets of paint to us every summer, and we could either put a coat of paint on the floors or on the walls. We couldn't even afford carpets or throw rugs; on a winter morning, those floors would be so cold that when our feet hit the floor, my four sisters and I would scream out loud.

But I had great friends growing up, and we had a lot of fun with what little we had. We'd play baseball, kickball, tag, hide and seek – anything that didn't cost anything to play. In the summer, we'd catch lightning bugs or race sticks down the street gutters.

There was always someone around to play with. I remember Bud Duckett, who was our resident inventor and a fantastic salesman. One time, he made a car that used wheels from an old wagon and a busted tricycle. He put a couple of wooden boards on the side, and he had a little cigar box for a trunk. I was the motor.

I pushed him around that neighborhood from daylight to dark. Bud was an innovator who was way ahead of his time, right up there with Fred Flintstone.

In the sixth grade, I received nothing for Christmas. I'd been waiting impatiently all year for the holidays to arrive, but somebody had stolen Christmas out of our car the night before. Two years later, a family called the Gazaways moved in across the street from us. Larry Gazaway was in my eighth grade class; everybody called him Mo.

After Christmas, Miss Colby went around the room during English class, and we all had to tell everybody else what we got as gifts. Mo stood up and said, "I got a pair of gloves, a 410 over-and-under shotgun, and a Roll Fast bicycle."

Then it was my turn. "Tony, what did you get for Christmas?" the teacher asked me.

I stood up. "I got to ride Mo's bicycle," I replied.

It was true. I did spend most of Christmas Day over at the Gazaways waiting my turn to ride Mo's bike. But what I really received from Santa that year were 500 pieces of Bazooka bubble gum and 12 quarters. And that's what I got for Christmas when I was in the eighth grade.

For all the fun we had as kids growing up in the projects, it was an often unnerving environment. Police patrol cars were a regular sight on my street, and occasionally we'd see our neighbors being handcuffed and led off – that's not something parents want their young children to witness. The ice cream man would turn off the music when he got to our block, because he was afraid of being robbed.

My parents, Claud and Bobbie Ingle, both came from humble beginnings. My dad only achieved a third-grade education. He went into the Navy as a teenager and after arriving back home, he worked at the Crown Cotton Mill for 25 years. He also toiled as a second-shift cab driver during the weekdays, and worked as a weekend bartender at a local watering hole called the Glenwood Tavern. He was a hard working man who believed that success was earned through sweat. He always told me, "Tony, work never killed anybody but it sure has scared a lot of them."

And he loved my mother. "Tony, your mother is a saint," he always said when I was growing up. "That's all you can say about her."

I always agreed with him on that point. Both of my mother's parents died when she was in the eighth grade, and she had to immediately quit school to help provide for her family after the tragedy.

Later on, she loved her six children with all her heart, and worked long shifts at the carpet mill to help feed and clothe all of us. Then she'd come home after work, and she'd cook and clean and do all the household chores. If friends or family needed help, she would always be the first one to come to the rescue. Visitors would come over to the house to chat with mom; even if she was extremely busy, she'd always drop what she was doing to provide a listening ear.

One thing my mother always resented, though, was my daddy's drinking. She hated that he spent so much time down at the "beer joint," and that he was so proud of his job there. "Claud, you aren't a bartender," my mother would say. "All you do is pop tops off beer cans and give them to drunks."

Alcohol was a regular feature of my early life. Once, when I was five years old, a visiting preacher came by our house on a hot July afternoon, trying to recruit folks to join his newly formed church. While he sat at the kitchen table reading scripture to my mother, sweat dripped off his forehead.

"Mrs. Ingle, I'm extremely thirsty," he asked politely. "Might I ask you for something to drink, please?"

Mother walked to the refrigerator and poured the preacher a glass of cold water. "I'm sorry," she said. "This is all I have to offer."

That's when I ran over to the refrigerator, pulled out daddy's last cold beer, and ran over to the table. I triumphantly held the bottle high in the air.

"Hey mom!" I yelled. "The preacher's in luck, we've got one left!" Mother told that story many times after that, and always said that the preacher gazed upon that cold beer as if it was the Mona Lisa itself. From seeing the look on his face, she knew that this fine upstanding man had definitely partaken of at least one "cold one" during his lifetime!

My mother always said I was the youngest bartender she ever knew.

My uncle B.F. Smith, my mother's brother, was a rough and tough guy. He was a brick mason by trade. I remember one time, he and some friends were playing cards and he caught someone cheating. B.F. pulled a knife on him and said, "I'll let some air out of you."

He once took my barbell weights and threw them through a car windshield. I don't really remember why he did that. And one thing everyone knew about B.F. was that you could ever, *ever* talk about the Korean War around him.

Legend had it that the initials stood for Big Fella. When B.F. came over to the house on weekends, he'd bring over a styrofoam ice chest. He'd say, "Tony! Here's five dollars. Go get that ice, take care of me now!"

I'd run out to get the ice, and he showed me how to do everything right. Get the bag of ice, drop it on the ground, break up all the ice, and fill up the chest with Pabst Blue Ribbon bottles. "Goosenecks" are what B.F. called them. I'd set them down in the chest.

"Get them gooses *cold* now!" he'd call out after me.

B.F. would be laying out on the couch, one hand in his pants, watching the baseball game of the week on the black and white TV. Curt Gowdy and Pee Wee Reese were the announcers in those days.

Then all of a sudden, out of nowhere, B.F. would yell out, "Tony! Choke me one of those gooses."

I'd go and retrieve a cold beer from the ice chest, as fast as I could.

"Let me see it smoke now!" he'd say. And I'd pop the top open in front of him to show him the vapor coming off the top of that bottle.

"Are there some of those little ice cracklings on the side?" he'd ask.

"Yes, sir, Biffy," I'd confirm.

And he'd drink that cold beer down. There'd be a little tear in the corner of his eye as he took that last gulp.

"Man! That was a *good* goose, buddy!" he'd say.

I was 11 years old at the time. I guess I really was the world's youngest bartender.

— — — — — —

I DON'T MIND HITTING BOTTOM, I JUST HATE DRAGGING

That same year, we were finally able to get out of the projects. My mother and father were making $200 a month between the two of them, and we could afford to rent a house near North Whitfield High School for $50 a month. Living so close to the school gave me the opportunity to watch football, baseball and track practices. I also snuck into countless basketball games without having to pay a dime.

In those days, I would play basketball whenever – and wherever – I could. I'd get on my bicycle and ride for miles over dirt roads just to shoot hoops with friends like Steve Joyce, Pete Perkins and Johnny Oxford. We'd play ball regardless of rain, snow or excessive Southern heat. When I couldn't ride my bike to their houses, I'd run, and there was a long way between houses out there in the boondocks. It felt like it took forever to get from one place to another.

I spent long nights shooting free throws in barns. I practically lived at the Dalton Recreation Center, where I played games all weekend long. And sometimes I even played in my bare feet.

In June after I had finished eighth grade, right after I was shut out of spring tryouts because my family couldn't buy me proper shoes, I helped Jake the custodian clean out the lockers at North Whitfield High. Helping old Jake out with cleaning and sweeping the gym turned into a regular summer job for me. He was a great guy, and that wasn't only because he had the keys to the vending machines. But I knew that if I worked hard, he'd give me a Coke and some cookies afterwards.

And it just so happened that when I was cleaning out a locker one day, I looked down to find a brand new Converse Chuck Taylor All-Star tennis shoe. It was a right foot shoe, size 10 1/2, and it was so clean and white.

I remembered what mom and dad always told me: never, ever steal. I didn't want to take that shoe, but school was out, and we were emptying out these abandoned lockers. Then I got to thinking. How many onelegged people did I know in school? I couldn't remember encountering anybody like that.

So I picked up that tennis shoe, and I hid it in a special place. I hoped and I prayed that I'd find the match somewhere.

An hour or two later, I was out back of the gym putting out the trash. I was 5-foot-7 and a hundred pounds soaking wet, so I had to climb on top of a broken desk to see over the top of the dumpster. I looked down in the trash... and lo and behold, I saw the heel of a white Converse tennis shoe.

"I hope it's a left foot," I said to myself. "Please let it be a left foot."

And then I did what any red-blooded American would do. I jumped up to the top of that dumpster and dove right in.

Much to my surprise, that dumpster was deep! As I navigated around in that ocean of trash, I was reaching and grabbing and looking and feeling, hoping I could find that shoe again. When I finally ran across that Chuck Taylor shoe, I grabbed it. It even had a shoestring attached; I was in luck! And what did you know, it was a left foot shoe... a size 9.

That's when I looked to the heavens. "Thank you!" I exclaimed.

It took me a while to wrestle my way out of that dumpster. After several failed attempts to jump out, I managed to escape. I immediately went back to get the right-foot shoe from my special hiding place, and then I ran home as fast as I could.

It was Christmas in June at the Ingle house! Sure, I might have worn size eight-and-a-half, but I had a size 10 1/2 tennis shoe to go with a size 9. As far as I was concerned, everything was just perfect.

I took the blue case off my pillow, and wrapped my new shoes up in the pillowcase. Then I put that package between the mattress and the box spring. It was a little bit lumpy, but that was okay. I lay down on that bed, crossed my legs, folded my arms back behind my head, and I just lay there. Those tennis shoes were the most valuable thing I owned, two tickets to my future and the keys to my dreams.

I was going to go out for the team in the fall after all, and I just lay there dreaming about playing basketball. I was going to be playing basketball for the North Whitfield Pioneers.

In the ninth grade, I made the freshman squad. I also made the B-team, as well as the varsity team. That was back before the rules were changed in Georgia to limit participation, so I played in nine games one week. I had a duffel bag with the Pioneer logo on the side, with home and away varsity uniforms, a freshman jersey and a B-team uniform in there. That bag was stuffed full.

At first, I got very little playing time in the varsity games. But I was able to play a lot for the B-team, and I started in the freshman games. Do you think anyone ever had to tell *me* to hustle? I pulled my shoes out of the trash. To this day, I hardly ever use the H-word. Hustle is just a given for me.

In December of my sophomore year, I put together a strong series of appearances off the bench for the varisty team. Coach Creel called me into his office.

"Tony, we're going to start you tomorrow night against Murray County High School," he said.

Murray County was one of the best teams in northwest Georgia. I never wanted to kiss a man until then (it never really was in my nature), but I almost went ahead and broke that rule for Coach Creel.

I ran home and told my sisters that I was going to start for the varsity team the next day. Bev and Kay and Sheila and Cindy were so happy, and my dear mother was beside herself with joy. But my sister Donna said, "Oh, no."

Donna was a cheerleader for the North Whitfield varsity team. "We're not *that* bad, are we?"

I waited up because I wanted to tell my father what had happened. He finally came into the house; it was pushing 11 p.m. and it was clear he'd been drinking. I could smell it on him.

He and my mother started arguing about finances. I tried to break up the quarrel by saying, "Mom, I'm going to give daddy the good news."

I told him that I was going to be starting for the varsity basketball team as a sophomore the next night.

"No, you're not, son," he said.

My father had got me a job down at the Evans & Black carpet mill making $2.75 an hour. "You're quitting school in the morning," he told me. "It's about time you start making your own way around here, and your family could use the help. Besides, all you ever do is play that [expletive] basketball, and it ain't going to get you anywhere." "Quitting school?" I replied. "I'm not quitting school!" Then I told him he was crazy.

You didn't talk back to Claud Ingle, especially when he'd been drinking a little bit. He didn't take too kindly to being shown up. So he peeled off his belt and whipped me. He told me that I was going to quit school, that I was going to do what he said, and that was the way it was going to be.

I remember him whipping me to the point that he was hitting me in the head with the buckle. Eventually, I blacked out.

The next morning, when I woke up, my whole body was sore and covered with welts. I had scars on my neck, my shoulders and on my legs. I'll never forget going to the bathroom that morning, where I saw the bloodstained towel that my mother had used to wipe the wounds of her son.

But I wasn't going to quit school. And I didn't. I didn't leave the basketball team either.

When they introduced me that night at the game, I had belt wounds all over my body. It was an embarrassing situation to be sure, and when you're a sophomore in high school, you don't want your friends (and especially the girls) to know you got whipped.

But none of that mattered when the announcer said for the first time, "And now, wearing number 15 for the Pioneers, Tony Ingle!"

I was no longer just a barefoot kid with a head full of ridiculous dreams. I had a jersey, I had a uniform, and I was somebody. There were a lot of better basketball players who wore that North Whitfield jersey, both before and after my time there. But I don't believe that any Pioneer player was ever more proud to wear that uniform.

After my junior season, there was an end-of-year banquet. My parents didn't go to the event, and they were at home when I returned in Billy Carlock's car. I brought three trophies into the house, and my mom was so happy. Then I went back to the car and brought back two more trophies. And another one. My mother was looking at all the shiny cups and statues, just laughing and clapping. She was so proud of me.

I looked out of the corner of my eye, and there was my father. He hadn't moved, he was just sitting there on the couch.

Billy came back to the house and said, "Tony, don't forget about this one." It was the seventh and biggest trophy of all, for Most Valuable Player. Billy set it on top of the television set.

My daddy got up, walked over to the TV, and took one look at the inscription: "*Most Valuable Player, Tony Ingle.*"

I thought that he might shake my hand, thought he might hug me, perhaps he'd even say he was proud of me. Instead, he said, "Well, that's alright."

Then he turned around, and sat back down on the couch.

During my senior year, in the middle of the season, the local paper wrote a really nice article on me. The writer noted that my father was Claud Ingle. A lot of people started coming up to him at work and asking him about me. And after that, daddy started coming to my games.

I'll never forget when we were in the middle of player introductions one night, three of us were standing out there at half-court. Just then, my daddy stumbled through the door of the gym. It was pretty obvious that he had been drinking heavily. I couldn't believe my eyes, I was shocked. One of my teammates turned to me and said, "Tony, isn't that your daddy?"

"Yep, it sure is," I replied.

"He looks like he's drunk as a skunk."

"Yep, it sure does."

"Aren't you embarrassed or ashamed?"

My father had taken time off from working at the tavern so he could come and watch his son play basketball.

So I said, "No, I'm not ashamed one bit. That's my daddy."

I was so full of emotion, and I felt this tremendous weight on my shoulders. My daddy was in the stands, and I wanted to show him how well I could play. I also knew in my heart that if my team lost or I played badly, he might never come to a game again.

I was hustling, scrapping, trying the best I could to win that game. Because of all my operations, my face would puff up when I'd sweat, and I would turn all red and pink because my facial pigmentation wasn't quite right. I remember getting on one of my teammates in a timeout huddle.

"You'd better go get some rebounds!" I screamed.

North Whitfield ended up winning that night. I never really was a very good shooter, but I remember what my daddy said when I got home. "The game was pretty good," he said. "But you need to shoot the ball more, boy. Every time you're open, you need to shoot that ball."

I had tried my best to please him, and I couldn't even do that. And I had 18 points in that game! But I realized that he had come to watch me, and that he had no concept of the kind of team game that basketball really is. My coach knew the game, and he taught me well.

I won the Most Valuable Player trophy again as a senior, averaging 18 points, 14 assists and nine steals a game. I nearly averaged a triple-double for the season.

North Whitfield won only one game when I was in the eighth grade, before they hired Coach Creel. We won nine during my freshman year, 10 the following season, and 15 in my junior year. When I was a senior, we won 21. So we were moving in the right direction.

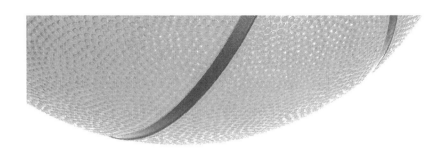

2

KANSAS SUNRISE

MY ONLY OFFER TO PLAY COLLEGE BALL CAME FROM Dalton Junior College and its head coach, Melvin Ottinger. North Whitfield had never enjoyed the kind of success it had during my senior year; we were getting a lot of attention for our breakthrough 21-win season. Coach Ottinger came to a lot of our games, and he signed me up with a scholarship.

I thought I was a pretty good basketball player, even though I was only 5-foot-9. I remember once in practice during my senior season, I was jumping up to retrieve a missed shot and I saw three guys' butts go past my line of sight. So I was grateful that Dalton took a chance on a little short guy like me. I was fortunate to join a program with such outstanding players, and I felt lucky to be on such a great team.

Our coach liked to do a lot of marketing and promotions; he was a real showman. At home, we wore a blue Chuck Taylor Converse shoe on one foot, and a white "Chuck" on the other. When we went on the road, we'd switch colors. And during my freshman year, it didn't matter which shoe was on which foot, because we beat everybody. We won 34 games in row, went undefeated, and Dalton was ranked second in the nation.

I didn't start on the team; I came off the bench instead. Because of my competitive nature, I always felt like I was better than the guy in front of me. Coach Ottinger didn't feel that way, so it was a tough time for me – I just wanted to play and help the team. But our team was winning, and Coach didn't want to mess with the formula too much.

We breezed to the Georgia Junior College Association state title. Then we went on the regional championship, where we had to play the winner of Alabama's state tournament to be named the best team in two states. We beat Walker Junior College from Jasper, Alabama, and Dalton was named Region XVII champion for the 1971-72 season. We earned the right to play for the national junior college championship in Hutchinson, Kansas.

The town was popping with pride. Everybody was so excited. Whenever we arrived at our home arena for games or practice, people would line up for autographs. The national tournament games from Hutchinson were played during the day, and back home in Dalton it was such a major event that the local elementary and high schools played the radio calls over their intercom systems. Everybody was tuning in on their radios to check up on us, and they were listening in on how well we were representing our hometown.

Unfortunately, our stay in Hutchinson wasn't a successful one, and Florida Gulf Coast Community College took us out in the first round. Our locker room was like a funeral home afterwards, with nearly everybody in tears. Our coaches had the tough task of snapping us out of our funk immediately, because we had another game to play the next day. We were slotted into a loser's bracket, and we had to restore whatever Dalton pride we could.

In that second game of the national tournament, Coach Ottinger gave me my first start. David Rainey, our primary point guard, turned his ankle in the loss to Florida Gulf Coast. Even though we missed our chance for the national championship, I was excited for the opportunity to show my coach what I could do. In my first-ever start as a college player, I scored 15 points, and we won the game.

I didn't play so well the next day, even though I scored another 15 points. Arizona Western defeated Dalton to send us home with a 35-2 final record. We did come home with a trophy, though, which officially signified that we were the 11th best team in the nation.

But I can't say that any of us returning players were very satisfied with 11th place.

My sophomore year didn't get off to a very good start. Before I went in for fall conditioning, I sustained a cut to my heel that required 14 stitches, so I started the season a bit out of shape. We had this routine where we ran up and down hills, and I remember puking my guts out during that exercise. I later broke the middle finger of my shooting hand playing football, and I kept re-breaking it as I kept playing sports.

I read in the local paper that Coach Ottinger said that the finger injury would likely cost me my starting spot. So I took off the brace and taped it up. I went into his office and told him it wasn't broken, and I even showed him the proof. It was my bird finger on my right hand, so I was basically giving my coach the bird. It was a little bit of attitude on my part, but that's the way I was at the time.

Coach never took me out of the starting lineup, and my teammates voted me captain of the team that season. I was playing the very best basketball of my career.

What's more amazing was that my mother and father came to nearly all of my games that year. Seeing my parents sitting in the stands, enjoying each other's company, and doing things together like a happily married couple did my heart so good. I was convinced that basketball helped bring them closer together again after all those years of fighting, and I was so very proud to have been a part of that.

And what a season it was. Our team were ranked as high as fifth in the national junior college polls, and we were treated like royalty on the streets of Dalton. We went on another long winning streak, and the only home game we dropped was the last game of the season. But we'd long since clinched our ticket to the playoffs by then.

We won the Georgia state championship for the second straight year, and we took the Region XVII title again to book a return trip to "Hutch" for the national tournament. I had a great game against the team from Alabama, but I had no idea at the time it would be the last juco game I'd ever play from start to finish.

After the game was over, I was putting on my warmups in the locker room. Neal Posey, the head coach at Huntingdon College, approached me and stuck out his hand.

"Hey, little man," he said. "I think you got robbed. You should have made the All-Tournament team. Did you know you scored 23 points out there tonight?"

I honestly didn't. "I didn't really come here to get on the All-Tournament team," I replied. "I came here to win the championship. I'm much happier about being on a championship team than if I'd won a trophy for myself."

"Oh, gosh, little man, I love that attitude," Coach Posey said. "*Man*, I get excited talking to you! Got a cigarette I could borrow?"

"No, sir," I said. "I quit smoking in the third grade."

He got a good laugh out of that, but it was the honest truth. When I was little, I'd retrieve cigarette butts out of my mother's ashtray.

In the third grade, I won a giant cigar at the county fair. I smoked half of that monstrous thing before I fell ill, and I was laid up in bed for three days. And that was the end of my illustrious smoking career.

— — — — — —

Dalton Junior College returned to Hutchinson for another shot at the national title, but this time things were very different. My father made the decision to take a week off from his job, and he borrowed $1,000 for the trip.

This was a complete shock on two levels: my dad never took any time off work, and only borrowed money when he needed it to fix our house or the car. My mom and sister Sheila came to Hutch too, as did my new girlfriend Jeanne Whitworth. Mom and dad didn't have a car that could survive a 16-hour drive, so they all loaded up in Jeanne's 1972 blue and white Ford Pinto. I was so happy and proud to know that four people I loved so much would be at the games.

I was so fired up, recalling all the events of the previous year – my first college start, our first defeat at the hands of Florida Gulf Coast, our blown chance to become national champions. In the days before that 1973 national junior college tournament, I dreamed and visualized that my family and Jeanne would all be part of Dalton's title celebration.

In the first round of the tournament, with eight minutes elapsed in the game, I stole the ball in the open court and started a speed dribble down the middle of the floor.

I glanced to my right, and there was my teammate Reggie "Taterhead" Smith streaking down the right side on the fast break with me. On my left, I saw Willie "Kip" Clawson filling the left lane. It was a threeon-two.

Normally in a situation like this, a pair of defenders will sprint back to the paint to form a tandem to protect the basket against two options, to try and cut the chances of scoring down to 33 percent. But during this particular play, one of the defenders jumped at me at half-court, trying to stop me from driving straight to the hoop.

My instincts took over. I swiveled and tried to perform a reverse-pivot, but he landed on my right foot. We both fell to the floor. That was a fairly common place for me to be – on the floor. Scratches, bumps and bruises were always part of my game.

But this wasn't an ordinary fall.

I twisted my pivot foot and took the full weight of the defender's body against me, and the impact tore everything out of my knee.

A hush came over the Hutchinson crowd. As I was writhing in painful agony near mid-court, I remember looking around in the crowd for my loved ones. I saw my dad, and I saw my mother too. I'll never forget the look on Jeanne's face – she was in complete shock. They all were.

Our assistant coach, Dick Coleman, says to this day that I kept screaming over and over, "I can go, I can go! Give me a shot. Shoot me in the knee with cortisone, anything. *Put me back out there, Coach!*"

I couldn't accept the fact I was injured. I'd always believed that being hurt is all in the mind. But I quickly found out that being hurt was in my *knee*. I jumped up and tried to run. I tried to shake off the injury so I could keep playing.

But I couldn't get my leg to move. I tried to hop on my left leg, but my right knee refused to flex.

The ligaments on both sides of my knee had been ripped apart, and the only thing that was left fully intact was my patella tendon. But I'd lost my mind to the point where my coaches and teammates had to grab me and restrain me before I did any more damage to my leg.

In the training room, it was obvious that courtside medicine couldn't do much for me. The trainer put my knee in a temporary brace – that was all he could really do under the circumstances. The staff made plans to fly me from Wichita to Chattanooga the next morning, so I could have emergency surgery.

During that last night in the Kansas hotel, I could hardly sleep. My teammates all came by the room to offer encouragement and consolation; for all their well-wishes, they could never heal me. I knew for certain that my basketball life would never be the same, and I had to come to grips with the very real possibility that my playing days were over altogether.

Basketball was such an important part of my childhood. It gave me purpose and direction as a young boy, and it became a crucial part of my identity. It united my family in a bond of love. Now it felt like basketball was being taken away from me.

We had to get up at 4 o'clock in the morning, and drive to Wichita so I could get on a plane and fly home. It was awkward showering and getting dressed, what with the giant brace on my leg and all.

I never will forget that morning. We drove in silence along the lonesome roads of Kansas before the sun came up. Clear golden light spread over the landscape as we continued onward.

Coach Ottinger was there with me. My dad was there, and mom and Jeanne had come along too. I remember feeling like I let each and every one of them down. I felt like our team had been good enough to win a national championship, and I wanted to share that moment with them so badly. But I felt like I had failed them all. My heart hurt worse than the knee did.

There was my dad, who never took days off from work and never borrowed money, who didn't even want me to play basketball five years earlier. Now he was getting wrapped up in my games.

Dad and Sheila were going to drive back to Dalton in Jeanne's car, so we said our goodbyes at the Wichita airport. And when we got to the plane on the tarmac, my daddy didn't say any words to me. He rubbed my head and walked away.

But I looked back and I saw him break down in tears. It was the first time I'd ever seen my daddy cry, and it broke my heart.

Then Jeanne, mom and I got on that plane and flew to Chattanooga. We were all crying. As the plane took off, I looked out the window and saw the sun peek out over the horizon.

Watching that slow sunrise in Kansas motivated me. I made a vow as the plane took off that day.

"One of these days I'm going to be back here," I said to myself. "I'm going to win a national championship for mom, dad and Jeanne. I'm going to make this up to them somehow. And if I can't do it as a player, I'll do it as a coach."

Nothing was going to get in the way of my dream - except for myself and my own human limitations. I vowed that no person, or any group of people, would ever stop me from achieving my dream.

No circumstances in the world would keep me from questing to get to the top.

— — — — — —

The surgeon at Erlanger Hospital in Chattanooga said my knee was the worst he'd seen in 20 years – and he had done two operations on an aging Joe Namath.

His first order of business was to strongly suggest to my mother that I never play basketball again. I'm no doctor, but it was described to me in vivid detail that I'd lost all the cartilage in my knee, and that my ligaments had to be tied back together. That was as good an explanation as I needed.

That knee still hurts me now, over a quarter-century later. There isn't a day that goes by when my body doesn't remind me of that injury in Hutchinson.

My teammates and coaches didn't forget about me while I recovered. At the postseason banquet, I received the team's "hustle award," the free throw award, as well as a bicycle to help me rehab my knee.

While I was in the hospital, Murray Arnold, the head coach at Birmingham Southern (who later coached Western Kentucky and the Chicago Bulls), recruited me. I was really honored that he thought I was still worth a shot.

But finally, I signed on at Jacksonville State University, a Division II school in Alabama. The team offered me a redshirt for the 1973-74 season, two years of eligibility, and most importantly a scholarship.

At Christmas, however, I left school and went home to Dalton. A lot of people told me at the time that I'd made a terrible mistake, but my heart wasn't 100 percent in it. The only thing I had going for me was my heart, and I didn't feel right doing something that I couldn't throw my whole heart into. My decision had nothing to do with my coaches or teammates; I didn't feel like I could ever again be the kind of basketball player I wanted to be.

Two years later, I returned to school at Huntingdon College in Montgomery for my junior year. When I wasn't studying, I was working evenings and alternating weekends at the Montgomery Boys Club. My official title was Physical Director, but the most important thing to me was that I was able to coach basketball.

The first team I ever coached was in a 10-and-under league. We went 10-2 for the season, and that really got my confidence up. Look out, John Wooden... that Tony Ingle can coach a little! Then, during my senior year at Huntingdon, I moved up a 14-and-under team and worked the 10-and-under games as a referee.

This was the west end of Montgomery, a rough area of town that had a lot of crime. That's why the Boys Club was there in the first place – to help keep kids off the street. Every Saturday morning, I had to kick the drunks out of the doorway so I could open up the place.

One night, I went into the gym and there was a grown man on a large trampoline double-springing little children, sending them high up into the air.

The kids were frightened, bouncing up all the way to the rafters and screaming their little lungs out. This guy was laughing at them.

So I told him to please get off the trampoline. "Hey, let them kids down from there," I ordered.

He jumped down and approached me menacingly. "You want some shit?" he asked.

And I replied, "*Whoa*, there!"

Then he pulled out a knife and snapped open the blade. I remember that he was a real quick draw.

"I'm gonna slice your guts out," he threatened.

I walked back towards the door of the gym. "Easy now," I said. "I'm not going to fight you. Put that knife down."

He kept coming towards me as I backtracked to the parking lot. I was driving that Ford Pinto that belonged to Jeanne, and I started backing towards the car.

I knew I had a two-by-four in the back seat. My plan was to get to the door, grab that plank of wood, and knock him clear into next week.

Well, when I reached in the door and put the seat-back down, he lunged at me with that knife. All my nerves went to my feet. My reflexes were quick enough to evade the blade, and I booked it down the street. I ran. Lou Brock had nothing on me, baby!

I could feel him right behind me, chasing me down. I quickly realized that I had no idea where I was going, and that he surely knew the area a lot better than I did.

I was on a dead-end street in Montgomery, Alabama, and there was no way out, but I noticed a stop sign up ahead. I was going to grab the signpost and swing around – just like in a Three Stooges movie – and high-tail it back to the Boys Club. But I was running so fast that I flipped over backwards when my arm hit that signpost.

As I hit the ground, I saw him standing above me, getting ready to slice my guts out. I was ready for the knife to enter my body. But just then, Boys Club director Mike Anderson grabbed him from behind, and Mike shook loose the knife from my attacker's hand.

The situation was taken care of. But that's when I realized that when I fell, I'd ripped my beautiful cream-colored corduroy pants.

What *really* ticked me off, however, was that the kids at the Boys Club would point at me and say, "There's the guy who ran away from Bolo!"

It turned out the guy's street name was "Bolo." I felt like so much less of a man, because I backed down from a fight with a guy whose name sounded like "Bozo."

— — — — — —

After graduating from Huntingdon in 1976, I had two days off. I finished school on a Friday and I went to work the following Monday.

My old high school, North Whitfield, merged and consolidated with Westside High, and they combined the two names. I was going back home, to the brand-new Northwest High School. Steve Jones was hired as the head coach of a team the school board decided to call the Bruins, and I was hired to be his assistant.

Early on, one of the parents came to me and complained that his son never got to play.

"I appreciate your time," I told him. "I definitely see where you're coming from."

Then I took the whistle off my neck, and offered it to him. "Now go take your son with you, and you go coach him on *your* team. Or leave me alone, and I'll coach him on *my* team."

The world's full of coaches, isn't it? A week or so later, another parent called me on the phone. She was really upset because her son wasn't starting.

After listening to her very politely, I began my response in the form of a question. "First of all, can you hear me?" She said yes, she could hear me.

"Do we have a good connection on the line?" Once again, she replied in the affirmative. "Do you have a whistle, ma'am?"

She said that no, she didn't have a whistle.

"OK, then you come down to my office and pick yourself up a whistle. Then you take him home and *you* coach him."

I was not going to let anyone run my program except Coach Jones and myself.

One kid on the team was a real hustler. I really liked him because he reminded me of myself. He scrapped, he clawed, and he left it all out there on the court every game.

And I remember walking into the locker room at halftime one night, and everybody was eating fudge. I only got fudge at Christmas! What's more, they each had a nice big bottle of Coke too!

I found out that the halftime snacks were provided courtesy of the parents of this fine young hustling ballplayer. I said, "Mr, Keener, if you don't mind, this ain't no dag-blang birthday party. We're trying to win a basketball game here!"

"But it gives them a burst of energy," he replied. "That sugar is good for them, and it'll help them perform better."

I didn't know about that. I kindly asked him to please wait until games were over to give out fudge and Coke to the players.

With six games to go in the season, I had to take his son out of the starting lineup because he wasn't hustling as much as he had before. After that, we didn't get any more fudge. I couldn't figure out why! Then Mr. Keener went to the Whitfield Board of Education and told them that I was a horrible coach and that I should be fired immediately.

I had a lot of friends on that board, and they all pretty much laughed him out of the room.

In the spring, I found out that Southeast High School, Northwest's crosstown rival, fired their coach. Southeast went 9-43 in his two years, and people weren't happy with the direction of the program. So I applied for the job, because I felt I was ready to step up from the assistant's role and become a head coach.

I was on a track, I was on a mission, and I was determined. I couldn't fulfill my dream of becoming a great college player, but I could become a great college coach someday. Becoming a high school head coach was my next step.

Jasper Rogers, the principal there, made the final decision to hire me. I never will forget when Bill Hargis from the county office called me and said, "I wanted to be the first person to congratulate you for becoming the next head coach at Southeast High School."

I jumped 20 feet in the air; I do believe I did. I ran around the house, and I was so happy. I was running around and high-fiving and hugging anyone and everyone I could find. I found Jeanne and hugged her. I was now a real live head coach!

But I knew, even back then, that the road to my dreams would be tough. I knew that there would be a lot of dark hours ahead. But when I got the job at Southeast, in order to remind myself to persevere through the tough times that would surely come, I wrote down a thought that I've carried with me to this day.

"Instant success has made a failure out of many," I wrote. "But long-struggling success has made a path for many to follow."

The first thing I did as head coach was hold spring basketball try-outs. This school won five games that year, and just four the year before. Southeast had lost over 20 games in each of those two seasons. They were so used to losing that I decided to give the team a little pep talk about winning. I had them all sitting there in the locker room, and I was really trying to fire them up.

"Define for me a winner," I challenged them. "Tell me who in this world is a winner."

I thought they'd say Vince Lombardi. John Wooden, maybe. This was 1977, so Tom Landry was in his heyday as the great and famous football coach for the Dallas Cowboys.

One kid who was trying to make the team slowly raised his hand.

"You, son," I shouted. I had a lot of momentum going, my eyes were popping out, and the veins in my neck were bulging. "Tell me who's a winner. *Tell me who's a winner.*"

"Oscar Mayer," he said meekly.

I remember looking at the kid as I heard all the others giggling to themselves. I had been so wrapped up in my pep talk, so I was struggling to place the name.

Who was Oscar Mayer, I thought? I couldn't place him. Was he a sprinter in the Olympics? Was he a long distance runner? A downhill skier? A tennis star? I was scratching my head.

"Who's Oscar Mayer?" I finally asked.

Then one of the other kids looked up at me and said, "Hey, coach, it's a *wiener.*"

That broke the tension in the room. Everybody fell over laughing, including myself.

Soon thereafter, I went to a baseball game at Northwest High School. As I was leaving the park and walking towards the parking lot, Coach Ross, the basketball coach at Trion High School, walked up to me and congratulated me.

"How's it look down there?" he asked me.

"This program is in real bad shape," I replied. "They've never won anything at Southeast, not a single trophy. And they've had some real problems. From what I can tell from the research I've done on the team, I'm going to have to run some of those kids off."

Coach Ross stopped walking, and paused for a second. He looked at me.

"What do you mean?" he asked. "What are you talking about, 'run some of those kids off?'"

"I've heard that couple of them are drinking and smoking, they might even be smoking dope too," I answered him. "I can't tolerate that. I'm going to run a tight ship down there at Southeast."

I'll never forget what Coach Ross said next. He looked me straight in the eye.

"Well, *that's* a bad attitude," he said.

"You're right, coach, it is a bad attitude, those kids shouldn't be doing those things."

"No, no, Tony," he replied, "It's not *them* I'm talking about. I'll say it again. *That's* a bad attitude."

Nobody had ever told me I had a bad attitude. I was taken aback. I had always prided myself on hustling and having a *good* attitude, and had tried hard to stay dedicated and positive.

He put his arm around me. "Now son, listen to me," Coach Ross said. "Those kids down there at Southeast... they did all that stuff under the other coach. They might not do that under you. And after all, what are you coaching for if you're not going to try and help kids?" *Wow*. That hit me like a ton of bricks.

I went home and really thought about what Coach Ross said. I thought about it all summer, and all during our first practices in my first year as the head boys' basketball coach at Southeast High School. As it turned out, I never ran off those two kids I was planning to kick off the team.

I had one simple rule I expected my players to follow. Even if it was snowing, sleeting or hailing, my players had better not miss a single practice. If practice was cancelled, I'd call them on the phone and tell them it was cancelled. But if they didn't hear from me, or if the phone lines were down, they'd better be at the gym at the designated time if they wanted to stay on the team.

It just so happened that it did snow one night. It was a horrible storm, with ice all over the roads. The phone lines didn't go down, so I called the players to tell them I was canceling practice. But these two particular young men were so poor that they had no phone at home, so I knew I had to go to the gym.

"There's no way you're going to the high school in this weather," said Jeanne, who had become my wife by then.

"Honey, I need to go if I have to walk," I replied. "Just in case."

I drove as close to the high school as I could get. I barely made it to the school parking lot, and walked all the way to the gym. And there I found those two boys, whom I'd once thought were too much trouble to keep on the team, huddled in the doorway.

Neither one had a coat on. I had no idea they had so little money they couldn't even afford winter clothes. They were nearly frozen to death, waiting for their coach to arrive and open the door.

As I drove them home through the snowy roads, I remembered what Coach Ross had told me the previous spring, and I smiled. The only thing these two young men had going for them was basketball, and I was glad I didn't take that away from them.

We played in the Murray County Christmas tournament. We won our first round game, and then our quarterfinal. Then we went up against Dalton High in the semis. If we beat Dalton, we'd make the finals, which would be pretty big news for a school with no conference, no trophies in the trophy case, and only nine wins over the previous two seasons. Dalton was ranked fifth in the state that year, too.

There was a defense I ran at Southeast that I called "Blue." Technically, it was a 1-2-2 three-quarter half-court press. So we were down by six points late, and this was back before the three-point shot, so it was a three-possession game. When Bobby Morrison hit a jump shot for us, I jumped up in the air and I yelled out, "Euuuuu!"

My team thought I yelled out, "Blue!" They immediately jumped into that half-court press, and we stole the ball and scored three times in a row. We ended up getting the lead and winning the game, and it was one of the greatest victories in the history of the school. And it was all because my team thought I said something I didn't. I love this game!

We lost the next night in the finals of the Murray County Christmas tournament. But Southeast ended up beating five state-ranked teams that year. We did get a little overconfident, which led to a valuable lesson for me. When we played Gilmer County High, I addressed my team before the game.

"These guys are terrible. We'll kill 'em."

Gilmer County beat Southeast that night, 88-87. I never took another team lightly again.

We certainly didn't win them all. I remember one game against Murray County High School. The game was already decided, and we were losing really badly. I started ranting and raving – this was the beginning of my long career of demonstrative behavior on the sidelines.

Frank Seabolt, who called the high school circuit back when I played, came over to me. I loved Frank, I always thought he did a great job calling games.

"Tony, calm down now," he said. "You're going wild over here."

"Hey Frank," I said. "I know I'm going crazy. And you know as well as I do that coaches do stuff like this in order to fire up their teams. But I want you to know something. For years, I've been wanting you to be the one to give me my very first technical foul. Ever since I decided to become a coach, I've been dreaming of the day that Frank Seabolt would ring me up."

Frank looked at me, and I could tell he was confused. But I just smiled at him. But he obliged. Frank Seabolt gave me my very first technical.

One of my star players was Eddie Monroe. He was a fierce competitor and a bit of a hothead, and he racked up 13 technical fouls the year before I arrived at Southeast.

At the beginning of the season, I called Eddie into my office and told him that there would not be any more technicals. He and I made an agreement that whenever he lost his temper, he would count to 10. Then he would look at me, and I'd try my best to calm him down a little bit.

That turned out to be a real case of the blind leading the blind... but it was a strategy, I suppose. But it turned out that Eddie made it through the year without a single technical foul.

In our last home game of the year, we were playing Kirkman High School from Chattanooga, Tennessee. Clyde Willocks, a great local basketball official and a friend of mine, came up to me before the game and said, "Tony, I want you to know that if Eddie can get through this game without a technical foul, we're going to give him our Carpet Capital Officials Association Player of the Year award. I'd appreciate it if you didn't say anything, I just wanted to let you know."

I was so proud of Eddie. "Man, that would be awesome," I said. "You have my word. I won't say anything to him."

The game started. It was immediately obvious that Kirkman was a better team, but we started cutting into their early lead. We were really battling all the way to the end.

Late in the game, Eddie jumped up and pulled down a key rebound, and about three or four opposing players surrounded him and started hacking his arms, mugging him.

When the ref blew the whistle, Eddie emerged, and I could see it in his eyes. He was *steamed*.

"Ohhhh no," I told my assistant. "Eddie's fixin' to belt somebody." And Eddie went right at one of the Kirkman players.

Then he suddenly stopped, put both of his arms down at his sides, and walked off. I knew he was counting to 10 in his head. And then he turned around and looked at me. I gave him a big ol' smile.

We lost the game, but Eddie won that award. After the post-game handshakes, Clyde came over and congratulated Eddie and I, as he had become the Carpet Capital Officials Association Player of the Year.

One certain fan in the stands wasn't so impressed. My father was standing behind me, berating Clyde for calling such a bad game. I wish I could print all the things he was saying, but I can't.

My dad was yelling at him about all the calls he had supposedly blown, all about how he was blind, how he was a mullet. According to Claud Ingle, Clyde needed to find a more appropriate line of work right away.

After a few minutes of this, Clyde had enough. "Tony, will you call security and get this guy off of me?"

I turned around. "Hey daddy, would you leave the nice man alone?" Clyde was shocked.

"That's your *daddy*?" he exclaimed. "I wish he was as good a sport as Eddie!"

We had a good laugh about that. I was happy for Eddie that day for controlling his temper on the court, but I was overjoyed that my daddy was there in the bleachers, with my best interests in mind.

3

SHAKE AND BAKE

IN 1978, AFTER I COMPLETED MY FIRST SEASON AS THE head coach at Southeast High School, I started looking for other opportunities.

At Southeast, we didn't play in a conference that gave our team preset home-and-home matchups. The only way we could get into the state championship tournament was to play well enough in our local region's tournament to get an invite. And we scheduled every game ourselves, which was hard work. We had to play a tough schedule full of tough teams, many of which we weren't familiar with.

So I looked into a few jobs around the Dalton area. But I usually saw right away that I was going up against much more qualified applicants. I didn't have much of a chance.

But one day, there was an out-of-the-blue phone call. It was Dr. Edwin Casey from Cherokee High School in Canton, letting me know that I had been highly recommended for the school's head coaching job.

In Georgia, there were four divisions based on school size – Cherokee was 4-A, the highest of the four, with over 1,700 students. There were 29 other applicants for the job, but Dr. Casey kindly invited me to put my name in.

"I've got permission from your principal to talk to you," Dr. Casey said. "I hope you'll consider coming in and talking to us."

I was very young – still in my mid-twenties – and that was a big topic of conversation when Cherokee interviewed me. The hiring committee was specifically worried about my ability to discipline players who were only seven or eight years younger than I.

"Let's just put it this way," I explained. "If I get to be your coach, I'm gonna be the daddy rabbit. I'll run this team and this program and nobody is going to push me around."

The daddy rabbit. That nickname stuck, a lot of people really liked that. "Tony Ingle might not be a head coach," one of the board members said

afterwards. "But he sure is a daddy rabbit!"

Gene Norton, a superintendent of schools in Canton and a Cherokee board member, came down to Dalton on business one day. He stopped by Southeast High School and visited with me.

"You interviewed for the job at Cherokee," he said to me as he entered my office. "I want to talk to you for a second."

"I've got a son whom I'd really like to play basketball," Gene explained. "He's not a very good basketball player, I'll admit that. But, you know, we have a lot of black boys there in Canton, and he's *definitely* not as good as they are.

"But I sure would like to see him on that team. You know what I mean, Tony?"

"Yeah, I know what you mean," I replied. "But I'll tell you what, Mr. Norton. You probably need to get another coach. I was 5-foot-7 and 100 pounds in high school, and if my coach had played favorites, I would have never made it out on the floor. I have a question for you. What are your school colors?"

"Red, white and black," he said matter-of-factly.

"That's all I see as a coach," I shot back. "I'm not going to put the superintendent's son on a team because of his skin. You'd best find another coach."

"No, no, Tony," said Gene. "My son doesn't even *play* basketball." It was a test.

"He's got two left feet," he admitted. "I wanted to make sure you were going to be fair to those black boys. They deserve a fair opportunity as anybody else, especially if it makes us a better team. You're awful young, and I know this a high-profile 4-A job, but I think we've found the coach we were looking for. What would you do if we gave you this job, Tony?"

I had my answer ready. "First thing I'd do is express my appreciation to you, Dr. Casey, and everyone who was involved in hiring me," I said. "The second thing I'd do would be to assure you that you'd made the right decision. The third thing I'd do is call my wife."

"You think things through, don't you, Tony?"

So Cherokee entrusted me with its head coaching job, and Dr. Casey handed me the keys to the gym. I remember walking into that gymnasium for the first time. Everything was painted green and brown.

There were two entrances to the gym. When I walked in on the side with the girls' locker room, I saw five state championship banners. There were smaller banners celebrating 22 regional championships in 25 years, and there was a "wall of honor" with plaques naming a slew of all-region performers. A few Cherokee girls went on to play for the University of Tennessee women's program, and a couple even played for the U.S. Olympic team.

There was a phenomenal legacy of winning basketball on display. I couldn't wait to get to see what the boys had done.

When I walked over to the other side, there were pictures, no banners, nothing. All I saw was a little wooden sign painted in black letters. It read, *"Please, No Food Or Drink In The Gym."*

I knew I had my work cut out for me.

There were big full-page ads in the local paper advertising the girls' games, but they never mentioned that Cherokee played home doubleheaders and that they boys' team played afterwards.

I rolled up my sleeves and built the program. But I didn't want to try to downplay anything that the girls had done. I've never believed that the way to build yourself up is to cut others down. I just wanted to let the community know that the boys had a basketball team too. I wanted to carve out our own identity.

I often talked to my high school coach Brady Creel during that time. He mentored me well, and he helped me build my coaching philosophy. Coach Creel taught me the importance of building a program with the fundamental building blocks of honesty, organization and proper delegation.

"Always go through the proper channels," Coach Creel always told me. "Never, *ever* fight the system. And always, *always* make them money."

It was obvious right away that people would come for the girls' games, and then leave. So what I did was teach our team a little Harlem Globetrotters routine that they'd perform during warmups. I was a gym rat in college, and I knew all those moves.

I taught the players how to roll the ball down their arms, spin it on their index fingers, bounce it between their legs, make fancy passes and do crazy stuff in the layup line. We even played "Sweet Georgia Brown" over the speaker system when we came out of the locker room.

And believe it or not, the crowds stopped leaving after the girls' games.

When our games started, they saw us scrap and hustle.

Then we started winning a little bit.

I was reading a book called *The Wishbone Offense* by Bob Fuller, and he wrote about how he had his players turn cartwheels. I had five sisters and four of them were cheerleaders, so I knew how to turn one myself. We had a big game coming up against the Eagles of Etowah High School, our main county rival, and I thought we'd install a cartwheel play in our offense.

I shut the gym doors and didn't let people outside see what we were up to. We were in there for two weeks practicing cartwheels. We called our play "Three," because if you hold up three fingers (like you might do while reciting the Boy Scout pledge) it forms a W, for "wheel."

Three was an inbounds play for when we were under the opponent's basket. Here's how it worked: the four players on the floor set up in a box; two were stationed down low on each block, with the other two at the "elbows" on each side of the key. The player on the ball-side block would turn a cartwheel. Then one man at the elbow would do the same, then the kid at the other elbow. The player on the weakside block would back-pick, and the original inbounder would come off that pick for a jumper.

The gym was packed for the big rivalry doubleheader with Etowah. Word got out around school that we had something special planned, and that they should really stick around after the girls' game for something fun.

At some point in the third quarter, after we had built a 10-point lead, the ball went out of bounds under our basket. From the bench, I held up three fingers. *Three!*

And we ran the cartwheel play. *To perfection.* John John Thomas took the ball out because he was the only one who couldn't do a cartwheel. As soon as Joey Groover turned one, the crowd gasped. Finally, Scott Blanton set the pick and John John knocked down the jumper.

The crowd loved it. I thought the gym was going to blow up! Coach Gastright from Etowah thought it was a lack of respect and sportsmanship, but I assured him after the game that I all wanted was to give the fans something to talk about.

The headline in the newspaper the next morning said, "*Warriors Cartwheel To Victory.*"

Then everybody started talking about the Cherokee High School boys' team. We hustled, we pressed, we trapped, we played together, we were fun to watch. And we turned cartwheels during games.

People who hadn't been to a game in years started showing up, wanting to find out what was going on at Cherokee. And who was this crazy new coach?

One night, we were playing Cartersville. We'd already run the cartwheel play against some other schools, so our reputation preceded us. Chuck Miller, Cartersville's coach, had won over 700 games in the state of Georgia. He had an outstanding program that had sent a lot of players to Division I colleges, and he had a very serious, all-business persona.

So during the game, we had the ball under our basket, and we called Three. The ball went around the horn, and we did the cartwheels. But we missed the shot, and Coach Miller immediately called time out. He ran down the sideline towards me and got right in my face. He was ticked off.

"There's no place for cartwheels in the game of basketball," he screamed at me. "Maybe you should take that stuff back to Dalton. This is quad-A, the big leagues. You're making a joke of the game, and you're embarrassing your school and yourself. Tell me, why would you want to do that for a cheap laugh?"

And I said very calmly, "Well, Coach, look at you. You're all stirred up and excited... I sure got inside your mind, didn't I?"

Later on, we were playing at Marietta High School. Charlie Hood was the coach there, a living legend in Atlanta-area high school ball. His team at the time featured Dale Ellis, who went on to the University of Tennessee and hit a lot of 3-pointers for the Seattle SuperSonics. A lot of people forget that Dale had a twin brother named Darryl, who was an exceptional athlete in his own right.

And *both* Dale and Darryl were on this team. Marietta was a powerhouse, ranked second in the state.

Marietta had us down by 25 points, and the game was winding down. I called time out, and everybody came running over to the bench.

"Guys," I said. "Remember what Bart Starr said about champions? He said that you can always tell a champion. No matter if he's up 30 down 30, he's still playing and giving the best that he's got. The game's never, ever over. Remember when he said that?"

"Yes, sir!" said all the players in unison.

"Well, this game's over," I told them. "We're getting beat like dogs."

They all looked at me, dumbfounded. A guy on my team named Russell Simmons spoke up. I loved Russell for being such a competitor.

"C'mon, coach, we can still win!"

"Nope, game's over," I repeated. "We're down 25 points with a minute to play, and there's no 30-point shot in the rulebook. We're beat."

"But here's what we're going to do," I said. "We're going to have some fun for the rest of the night. We're not going to let them destroy us. We're not going to be down and out and unhappy because they beat us like a bass drum. We're going to leave here *happy*. So who wants to bloomerleg one?"

The players were stunned. They didn't know what I was talking about.

"Ummm, coach, what's a bloomer-leg?" asked Russell.

"You get the ball, you put it down between your legs," I explained. "Just like Rick Barry shoots foul shots. Then you underhand that ball with all your might up towards the rim. Now who wants to bloomer-leg one from half-court? Kevin Foster, what about you?"

Kevin was kind of a shy kid. "Welllll," he said tentatively, before his face broke out in a big smile. "Okay, I'll do it."

I knew Marietta was going to sit in that 2-3 zone and stay off our shooters, so I had Kevin dribble the ball up to half-court where it said "M.H.S." in big letters. He looked over at me, and I gave him a little wink.

"Let 'er fly, big man," I said.

And he took the ball and put it down between his knees. Then Kevin Foster bloomer-legged it from half-court. When that ball hit the rim, my whole bench stood up in anticipation. They thought it was going in. But it rattled off the iron and bounced out.

Robert Thomas grabbed the offensive rebound, and dribbled out to the top of the circle. Then he bloomer-legged one too. That shot almost knocked a hole in the backboard.

The game was over. Marietta won by 25, but we had made our statement. The other team won the game and embarrassed us, but we weren't going to let them ruin our lives. We weren't going to leave that gym feeling sorry for ourselves.

———————

When Marietta came back to our place, we had another little surprise in store.

A few days before our rematch, I called my starting five together in a huddle before practice. I drew up a new inbounds play on a chalkboard.

"Guys, here's what I want you to do," I said. "Dennis Trimble, you're going to take the ball out of bounds. Dorrence Powell is going to stand at the ball-side block. John John Thomas will be at the elbow, and then we're going to have Joey Groover and Scott Blanton on the weak side."

"Now, pay close attention," I continued. "John John's gonna turn a flip. Dorrence, Joey and Scott are going to all fall down and start jerking and shaking like they're having seizures. Then Dennis is going to throw the ball to John John and he's going to drive to the basket and score."

I got down on the floor and started jerking and shaking. I showed my tongue.

Then I got up and said, "That, right there, is what we're going to do in the ballgame."

The players were speechless.

Finally, Scott said, "No way, Coach. Cartwheels are one thing... I'm not doing *that!*"

"C'mon, Scott, this is something you can tell your grandkids about," I said. "We're going to call this play Five, because it takes all five players committed to do it. Now, we're going to try this in practice against the second unit. I'll put them in a 2-3 zone. When I call Five, run the play."

And when we sprung it on the second team in practice, the play worked perfectly. Scott even came on board when he saw how much fun it was.

I swore everybody to secrecy. Nobody was going to tell anybody anything if they wanted to get any playing time against Marietta.

"I'll kick you off the team if you tell anyone," I said. "Just tell all your friends to be in this gym on Friday."

Game day arrived. The gym was packed, and you couldn't get a peanut in there unless you carried it in your pocket. The intensity... you could cut it with a knife.

We were hustling and scrapping. Before I knew it, there was 2:30 left in the game and we were behind by only five points.

And I forgot all about the play.

We had the ball under their basket and called time out. In the huddle, Tim Mainord, the freshman team coach, piped up.

"Hey, Coach," Tim quietly whispered. *"Run Five."*

I had only designed Five because I thought Marietta was going to blow us out again. I never said that to my players, but I knew that this team had already beaten us by 25. What's more, they were probably looking to beat us by 50 because of the whole bloomer-leg incident. In my mind, Five was supposed to represent a little bit of defiance against a far superior squad.

"What in blazes do you mean?" I asked, my face red and hot. "We have a chance to win this game!"

I looked at the players, and they looked so hurt. They wanted to show the fans the new play they had worked so hard on.

"C'mon, coach," said Scott. "You've told us all along we could win this game. Everyone in the stands knows that we made a special surprise trick play for them. Please, Coach, let us run Five."

My heart dropped to my ankles. I thought I was on my way to losing my job for running a gimmick play and blowing our chance to beat the second-best team in the state.

But I knew they had me.

"Okay," I relented. "We'll run Five. But let's put a full-court press on just in case we miss the shot."

But in my mind, I was saying, "I'm going to get fired tomorrow morning. Maybe even after the game. That's it, I'm fired. I'm going back to Dalton. It's all over. I just know it."

The team was so happy and pumped up, and they charged out on the floor. The referee handed Dennis the ball.

My heart stopped.

I couldn't watch.

But then I figured that if I was going to be terminated, I might as well watch my demise first-hand from my front-row seat.

Okay. Now, what would you do if the guy you were guarding in a basketball game dropped to the floor, then started having a seizure with his tongue hanging out?

I'll tell you what Dale Ellis – a future NBA All-Star and a fine gentleman – did. Dale bent down to help Scott up off the floor. When he hunched over, John John jumped clear over him, and laid the ball in for two points!

The radio announcers for the game were Byron Dobbs and Les Conley. This is what the call sounded like, and the local radio station replayed it every day for two weeks.

> BYRON: Ladies and gentlemen, here we are with 2:32 to go in the fourth quarter, Marietta up five. Cherokee's taking the ball out. Trimble with the inbound, Marietta in a 2-3 zone. Oh... oh! WHOA! What happened? They're on the floor! Cherokee players are all over the floor! And there... WHOA! Thomas has scored for Cherokee! And... it's a steal... and another basket for Cherokee High School! The lead is down to one! Coach Hood is running to half-court, time out, time out! There are people everywhere! Coach Ingle's left the building! This is unbelievable, I've never seen anything like this! What is going on here? Les, what's happening, Les?

> LES: I... I don't know, Byron! I'm speechless.. I...

> BYRON: They're trying to get the crowd off the court! I can't believe this! What kind of play was that?

LES: *It looked like a* dead cockroach *play, Byron!*

The roof came off that gym.

Pandemonium broke out. The referees were stunned. The Marietta players were stunned. After we ran Five, we put that full-court press on, and we stole the ball and scored again. Coach Hood ran out on the floor calling time out, and that's when some kids from the stands started streaming out on the court like we'd won the national championship. People were running everywhere.

I jumped up in the air, pumped my fist, and hollered, *"Yesssss!!!"* My assistant coach Ron Smith picked me up in a bear hug and ran me out of the gym into the lobby.

But the game wasn't over.

We were still down by one point with two minutes to go. And once the officials finally cleared the floor and restarted play, we ended up getting beat by 12 points. They made their foul shots, and we didn't - that's all there was to it.

After the game was over, our fans made a victory line that stretched all the way from our locker room, through the gym, into the lobby, and out the main door. Everybody wanted to congratulate and high-five our players. It was victory in defeat.

There was an elderly gentleman who came to all the games; his name was Hampton. He was dead drunk.

"Hey Coach," he said, his words slurred beyond recognition. "That's the damndest play I've ever seen. Run that shake and bake play again. One more time, Coach!"

Dr. Casey would come to ballgames a lot, and he'd sit there on the end of our bench near the water bucket. I had no inhibitions on the sidelines, and it was not uncommon for me to fake like I was drawing a charge. I jumped up on the chairs and did little dances. I never did it for show. I was just so wrapped up in the games.

But I think that Dr. Casey sat by the water tank just to keep a close eye on me.

During one particular game, I got excited and I started going down the bench to each player, slapping hands as I went. "Gimme ten," I said. "Gimme ten! Gimme ten!"

Then I reached Dr. Casey. He liked to do a lot of woodwork, and he had a bandsaw that cut off one of his little fingers. So when I got to him, I didn't miss a beat. He held out his hands, and I rolled up the little finger on my left hand. "Dr. Casey, gimme *nine!*"

We all laughed. Basketball was real fun back then at good ol' Cherokee High School.

One time, I got too cute. I couldn't resist. During introductions at our next game at Etowah, I had the guys turn cartwheels as their names were called. One of my guys' arms gave out, and he was out injured for a while. We got beat pretty bad that night, and I went to shake Coach Gastright's hand, he turned a cartwheel.

"Put 'er there, pal!" he said.

It was all in fun, but it made me a little bit uneasy. Perhaps I was becoming more of a clown than a coach.

Dr. Casey pulled me into his office soon thereafter. "Tony, could I talk to you?"

"Tony, your inventive plays have been good for us," Dr. Casey said. "They really have. But I look at things like the cartwheels and the 'shake and bake' play as good books. Sometimes you've got a good book and you don't want to put it on the shelf. But sometimes you have to go ahead and do just that. Isn't that right, Tony?"

"Yes, sir," I said softly. I understood.

"I'm not telling you how to coach," he continued. "But if you don't want to run the cartwheels, then that's just fine with me. Let's not do it for a while, okay? But if you want to sometime, just take that good old book off the shelf."

He didn't need to tell me twice. I put all those plays on the shelf. They had served their purpose. We ended up winning 10 games and losing 14 in my first year at Cherokee, but we had definitely got people's attention.

— — — — — —

Cherokee finished with a 18-6 record in my second year, and we won all 11 of our home games. It was the Cherokee boys' team's first subregional tournament berth at the 4-A level. We won 19 games the season after that. In my fourth year, we won 23.

In my fifth year as head coach, I called our starting five our "Fantastic Five," and they were some very special players. Our tallest starter was 6-foot-1, and that normally doesn't get it done.

Our leading scorer was Robert Thomas; he averaged 22 points a game that year. Keith Satterfield was our defensive specialist, and he was always getting key steals. Stell Morris came from a single-parent home and didn't start playing ball until high school. David "Goose" Cagle lived on a farm and got up at 2 a.m. to milk cows, and he still had energy left over for basketball. Our point guard was 5-foot-9 Billy Criswell, who almost quit hoops three years earlier because everyone said he was too little to play.

Those kids played their guts out for me. I have never coached a more determined and selfless bunch of kids before or since. Those players loved each other like brothers, and it brought me to tears sometimes during the season. I pushed them so hard to be their best, and they always responded with 100 percent effort and zero percent excuses.

We had an up-and-down regular season. But when we got to the regionals, that's when we really started playing well. Cherokee earned the right to play for the 1982 state championship by making it to the finals of our 17-team region.

It was the first time in two decades that the team had made it as far

as the state tournament. We traveled down to the Alexander Memorial Coliseum on the campus of Georgia Tech, also known as the "Thrillerdome." We got a great send-off from our fans as we boarded the bus. We were a country school getting ready to do battle with the best city teams; it was like "Hoosiers," but with thicker accents.

Cherokee played its first round game against Shamrock High School, which was coming off a 22-point win in its regional championship game. We, on the other hand, lost to Campbell High in the regional finals by 22. So I told the players that we were down 44 before the game even started.

We controlled the tempo and beat Shamrock, 65-57.

Then we beat Morrow High school in the quarters by executing our game plan perfectly. And there we were in the Georgia 4-A final four.

In the semis, we played Laney High from Augusta, a team that had gone 26-2. We played from behind all night, and finally pulled ahead in the final minutes. Staying out front against such a talented team was a real struggle, though. With 33 seconds to go, a Laney player hit a 10-foot jumper that signaled a huge momentum swing. The Wildcats came out at us with extreme pressure defense, trying hard to steal the ball away.

I don't really remember how we were able to keep possession on that trip down the floor. Robert Thomas had the ball knocked away, but it somehow deflected to David "Goose" Cagle. With a man right in his face, Goose launched a shot that arced so high that it could have hit the ceiling of the Thrillerdome on the way up.

As the ball was on its downward descent, the buzzer sounded, and it swished through the basket. Everybody piled on Goose at center court. That farmboy was the big hero that day. Cherokee was on to the state championship!

Campbell of Smyrna had lost in the state finals the year before, and they had four returning starters. In a word, they were mad.

Campbell came from our region, and beat us four times during the 1981-82 regular season. They had a 6-foot-9 guy, who was listed at 240 pounds, but my guess is that he was more like 290. We were so undersized that they could lob the ball inside to the big guy every time they wanted to.

Our team simply wasn't able to press and trap the whole game like we usually did. They were better and more athletic than us; that's all there was to it. The previous time we played them, they thumped us by 22 points.

We didn't start out that game well at all. With 2:40 remaining in the game, the score was Campbell Panthers 63, Cherokee Warriors 46.

We were down 17, and I called time out.

Most of the time in basketball, that's a clear signal that the coach is ready to wave the white flag and start bringing in the bench players. It's also a convenient time for fans to start gathering up their belongings and head for the exits, so they can beat traffic and save gas.

But that's not how I saw it. I told my team that we were going to win that game. With quick shots and pressing defense, I said, we could erase the lead and win the state title.

I challenged the players to strap on their boots and get to work.

Cherokee cut the lead to nine with 1:55 to go. With 57 seconds remaining, it was 65-58. Goose scored a putback off a rebound at 40 seconds, and we were down by six. Then we converted a three-point play with a free throw and came within three. With 14 seconds to go in the Georgia state final, we were behind by two points, 67-65.

I tried to stop the clock somehow, but I had used all our time outs during our comeback from 17 points down. So we called a time out anyway, and were assessed a technical foul.

Back then, this was a one-shot technical, and the shooting team would get the ball back. Panther player Darryle Bedford was an awful foul shooter, and he missed the single shot; we fouled him on the inbound, and he missed his first free throw of a one-and-one to give us the ball.

Then we ran the length of the floor, and Robert Thomas scored on a 15-foot jumper to pull Cherokee within a single point.

We figured that the strategy worked once, so why not try it again? I called another time out I didn't have, and Bedford missed another technical foul shot. But we were too slow on the inbound and couldn't hack him quickly enough.

The final score was 68-67, and Campbell won the state title that had eluded them the year before. But we had outscored them 19-5 in the final two minutes and 40 seconds. We didn't quit.

(As an aside, the Georgia High School Association rewrote the rulebook that summer. After 1982, a bench technical assessed for a non-existent time out became a two-shot situation instead of a one-shot opportunity. It became known in the state of Georgia as the "Tony Ingle Rule.")

After a state championship game, it's customary for the title winners to have a team picture taken at center court and then take a victory lap around the court. Once the Campbell players and coaches had completed their lap, after they accepted their trophy and lifted it high, I told my players to take a lap too. I told them they deserved to.

A member of the GHSA came up to me and said, "Coach, you can't do that. That's only for champions."

I looked him in the eye and replied, "Well, you'd better get off your butt and stop them then."

Our Cherokee Warriors, state runner-ups, paraded around the court. The entire crowd stood up and gave our team a standing ovation, even the Campbell fans. The Campbell players and coaches applauded too, showing their appreciation for the grit and determination of that little undersized team that came within one point of the state title.

In the locker room after the game, I met Bobby Cremins, who was coaching the Georgia Tech Ramblin Wreck at the time. He'd watched the whole game, and told me he was blown away at how my players had battled so hard against the odds. We hit it off immediately, and became fast friends.

Little did I know that my friendship with him would become one of the most important in my life.

—————

In addition to my coaching duties, I was teaching health and safety at Cherokee High School. I was earning my master's degree in education at North Georgia College, mostly so I would be able to coach at a college someday, but I was putting my experience to good use in Canton.

At that point of my life, coaching was getting me notoriety in the newspapers, but teaching was putting food on the table and paying the bills. I taught from 7:30 a.m. to 3:30 p.m., coached from 3:30 to 6:30, and was taking college classes at night. At 4:30 a.m. I ran a 55-mile paper route for the *Atlanta Journal-Constitution* – I did that for four months.

And then on Saturdays, I would officiate games, sometimes up to eight per day. I was burning the candle at all four ends.

One day at Cherokee, a guy knocked on my classroom door. It was Floyd, a student of mine. He hadn't been in school for a while, so I asked him how he was doing.

"Coach, I came to clean out my desk and locker," Floyd said. "I'm going home, and I won't be back."

"Floyd, where are you transferring to?" I asked.

"I'm not transferring," he replied. "Coach, I just got back from the doctor."

That's when I noticed that he had some blue marks around his neck. He looked awfully pale.

"I'm dying with cancer," Floyd continued. "My doctor tells me that I have six months to live."

I was shocked at what I was hearing. Here was a 14-year-old kid in the ninth grade, telling me he was dying. And he was as calm as he could be, explaining his condition.

I'll never forget what he told me next. He said, "Coach, I wanted to come by and I wanted to see you because I wanted to tell you that you were my favorite teacher. You always make me laugh. A lot of kids at Cherokee are going through tough times, you know, promise me that you'll keep 'em laughing."

I started to cry. Floyd and I hugged each other, and he started walking down the 100 hall of Cherokee High School.

For weeks after that, I couldn't think straight. I kept thinking about Floyd. I couldn't believe that he would never get to play football or basketball or baseball again. He wouldn't go to any dances, and he wouldn't get married or have kids. My last memory of him was walking down the hall, taking it all so gracefully.

My wife noticed that I was disturbed. "What's wrong with you?" Jeanne asked me.

I remember telling her, "I can't get my mind off Floyd." "Well, Tony," she said. "How long does he have to live?" "Six months," I answered.

"How long are you going to live?"

"I honestly don't know the answer to that, Jeanne."

"Floyd just might outlive you," she said. "We're not guaranteed any tomorrows. None of us are."

I really started thinking about the seriousness of life after that, about how short it really is. I thought about the decisions we all make every day, and how important each really is.

Floyd didn't make it as long as he thought he would. The cancer took him away after just three months.

But he had a real impact on my life. Floyd helped me realize the real importance of what I was doing: teaching kids. To this day, I've always tried to honor my promise to always keep 'em laughing.

4
THE LITTLE NUGGETS

AT THIS POINT, I SHOULD PROBABLY BACKTRACK A little bit. Between dropping out of Jacksonville State and moving to Montgomery, where I went to school at Huntingdon College and coached at the Boys Club, there was a two-year period during which my heart and mind were in the wilderness and not focusing on my future.

I was completely out of basketball for those two years. I was out of college, bumming around Dalton, trying to figure out what to do with my life. I had this crazy dream about being a basketball coach and winning a national championship, but I didn't know where to start. I didn't have a college degree, I didn't know many people in the coaching profession, and I had no real prospects. Jeanne and I had been dating for two years while I was at Dalton Junior College, but she moved out to Utah to work at the Church of Latter Day Saints offices.

While I was in Dalton, I ran into so many people who knew me from high school and junior college.

"Man, you're crazy for coming back here," they told me. "I really thought you were going to make it. You had so much fire and passion for the game. What happened to you? You're too good not to be involved in basketball."

I thought a lot about where I was going in life. I was usually accompanied by a cold beer, as I tried to figure out what my priorities were. I didn't know who I was. All I saw in the mirror was a 5-foot-10 point guard with a busted knee.

I thought about abandoning my dreams completely and following in the footsteps of my daddy. I figured I'd spend the rest of my days working in the carpet mills.

But it took me two years to learn an important lesson: we are our habits. And the greatest habit a person can ever have is to finish everything they start.

I don't make promises. I never even use that word. But I learned to pride myself as a finisher, as someone who never quit. I didn't care what anyone else said – I was going to complete every task I set out for myself. There have been many times when quitting entered my mind, especially during some of my later episodes in the coaching world, but I always came back to that one word: *finish*.

One thing I finally realized was that I had to get my butt back in college. I had to finish my degree so I could be a high school coach, so I'd be able to teach classes during the days.

The other thing I realized was that I loved Jeanne. I badly needed her in my life. I called her out in Utah, and I asked her to marry me over the phone. I was so lucky and fortunate that she said yes.

So Jeanne moved back to Georgia to be with me, and we had a beautiful wedding. Then we moved down to Montgomery. While I went to school and coached kids, Jeanne worked at the Wide World Health Spa.

I was really nervous when Jeanne was pregnant with our first child. There was no ultrasound back then, so we didn't know if it would be a boy or a girl. Because I was born with a face deformity, I had a lot of anxiety that something congenital would happen. I thought that my child would end up looking like me. I didn't want any son or daughter of mine to have to go through what I did as a child. Jeanne chose natural childbirth, so I was worried about her too. I loved her so much, and I loved that she had seen past my physical appearance to fall in love with me too.

When Eliott was born, his umbilical cord was caught around his neck.

I was terrified that he was going to be strangled, but the doctor got to work quickly. I remember the doctor started singing that old Ray Stevens song, "Everything is Beautiful."

It was a spiritual moment, the likes of which I'd never experienced. Seeing that perfectly healthy baby boy, with ten little fingers and ten regular toes (and a perfectly normal face) changed my life forever.

As I finished up my degree, Jeanne went back to Dalton with baby Eliott to find us a place to live. I didn't attend my graduation, because I was too busy packing.

But I'll never forget how my daddy came down with his truck to help me move my stuff back to Georgia. He always meant well, bless his heart, but he cussed me out for the entire two-hour trip. I was getting blasted.

"It took you five years to go to college," he yelled at me. "What a waste of time. In those five years, you could have been making at least $10,000 a year. You're $50,000 in debt from all those student loans now, and you're going to be in debt for the rest of your life. You and that damn basketball. One of these days, they're going to let the air out of that damn ball. What are you going to do then? Huh?"

For the next two years, when I coached at Northwest and Southeast, I made $8,500 a year. I remember telling Jeanne that I couldn't believe that I was finally being paid to coach.

"No, you're not," she wisely pointed out. "You're getting $8,000 a year to teach, and $500 to coach. Can you imagine living on $500 a year?" As always, she was right.

And our family was growing, too. By the time I was finished with my eight-year tenure at Cherokee High School, we had five wonderful children.

After Eliott, Jeanne and I had a beautiful daughter we named Sunshine. And then came three more handsome sons: Golden, Tony, and Israel, the youngest of them all.

— — — — — —

After we came within a point of the state championship, I stayed on for three more years at Cherokee High School. We had a few more good years, but we never could recapture the magic of that 1982 season and the "Fantastic Five." The Warriors didn't return to the Georgia 4-A tournament while I was there, no matter how hard we tried.

From a professional standpoint, I was ready to make the next move up the coaching ladder and land myself a college job. I networked as much as I could. I shook every hand I could find that was attached to a basketball coach. I worked camps during the summers, and volunteered my time at the Atlanta Tip Off Club.

In 1985, a coaching friend of mine tipped me off to Gordon College, which was restarting its program after abandoning basketball for 15 years. This was a two-year school located in Barnesville, Georgia, an hour's drive south of Atlanta. I seized the opportunity to apply.

But when I called athletic director Dave Chappel, he told me that they were already going to sign a new coach the next morning. He told me I could still send in my résumé if I wanted to.

I called up my friend Terry Lenahan. "They want me to send in my résumé?" I complained. "But they've already hired somebody!" "Go ahead, send it in," Terry said. "What do you have to lose?" "I don't have any money," I said.

It was true, I had only about $8.40 in my pocket at the time, not enough to send a Federal Express overnight envelope.

So Terry loaned me 13 dollars. It was nothing to him, but it meant everything to me. He and I worked quickly to get the package to the FedEx office in time, and we made the cutoff time by *that* much.

The next morning, I called Dave to check if they had received my Federal Express package. He told me it had indeed arrived, and noted that my résumé was very polished and impressive. But he said that he was very sorry about the timing; he was still planning to offer the job to this other coach within the hour.

Later that afternoon, Dave called me back. He wanted to see if I could come down the next morning at 10 o'clock and discuss the opening with his hiring committee.

I learned many years later that the meeting that morning didn't go so well. The coach they initially wanted to hire was a guy in his early twenties, who was just out of college. Dave asked this young coach, point blank, if he could handle black athletes. The answer wasn't what Dave wanted to hear. So Gordon College backed off, and decided to give me a shot at the job.

I walked into the office with a green coat on. It looked like I had just won the Masters! I don't remember where I found a coat like that, but I wore it. The school colors were green and white, and I knew exactly what I was doing. Dr. Jerry Williamson, the president of the college, loved it.

"Tony, what's your weakness?" Dr. Williamson asked me.

"I didn't come to talk about my weaknesses. I came to talk about my strengths," I said. "But I don't drink, cuss or smoke. Sir, I guess my weakness is that I work too much."

That sounded good to them.

I was hired at a salary of $23,000 per year as a coach and an associate professor. I was given the gym for two weeks during the summer months to run my basketball camps. After a full decade in high school ball, I was a real bona fide college coach.

In my darkest hour, after I got hurt at the national junior college tournament in Hutchinson, Kansas, I vowed that I'd lead a team to the national championship as a coach. I was hoping that it would be in "Hutch," and this was my chance to go back as a junior college coach.

Gordon College gave me a $3,000 budget to work with, and I ended up spending $2,900 on uniforms. The school hadn't fielded a basketball team in 15 years, and there were no uniforms around. I used the remaining $100 to buy a case of tape.

I had no scholarships to offer, so I really had to sell the new program to players. I thought the way to go was high-energy, high-excitement uptempo basketball. I called my offense "Wendy's."

Recruits would always tell me they'd never heard of that offense before, so I'd give them a simple explanation.

"You've ever heard of that restaurant, Wendy's?" I'd ask a potential Gordon College prospect.

"Yeah, Coach," he'd reply.

"Do you know why I named my offense after Wendy's?"

"No, Coach, why?"

"Because we're gonna *get it to go*, baby," I'd say. "Cheese on the fries, let it fly! I'm gonna get out of your way and let you play. We're going to wheel and deal, and give the crowd a thrill. I'm telling you, if somebody don't shoot that ball within 15 seconds, somebody's coming right out of the game!"

We were the Runnin' Gunnin' Generals – that's what we called our team at Gordon College. And we averaged 92.9 points per game that first year. The next year we went up to 94, and in my third year we were hitting 97. We pressed and trapped and made sure every single fan left the gym entertained.

We were gettin' it to *go*!

In my three years at Gordon College, I wasn't only the head men's basketball coach. I was a jack of all trades. I taught five classes (including archery) and I drove the team bus to road games. I washed the uniforms, swept the floors, and acted as primary fundraiser for the program. I even pumped up the basketballs with air before the games, and at halftime as well. I always had to hurry up with my locker room speech, because I had to pump the balls up – otherwise, the visiting team couldn't warm up for the second half. And since I never had a paid assistant coach, I did all the scouting, scheduling and recruiting too.

And was only one of my two full-time jobs.

— — — — — —

A modern-day spiritual leader named David O. McKay once said, "No other success can compensate for failure in the home."

I've seen men who run huge corporations, business and companies who cannot take care of their own families. The most important thing in life is to take care of your family. Family is the strongest unit on earth, as well as humanity's greatest team. It's definitely not the Green Bay Packers or the New York Yankees.

When my son Golden was a baby, I used to hold him in my lap and we'd watch basketball games on television together. We'd watch the Boston Celtics play. When Larry Bird hit a 3-pointer, I'd throw Golden up in the air and catch him! Then I'd move his hands so he was shooting, just like Larry.

I had that little guy in my lap dribbling and blocking invisible shots like a pro. Then, when he grew up a little, I gave him a real ball. He started dribbling at a very early age, and he had an excellent shooting touch.

Once, when Golden was three years old, I took him to an Atlanta Hawks game. Afterwards, I was waiting around to talk to Mike Fratello, who was Atlanta's coach at the time. While I was standing on the court, Golden found a ball and started doing some fancy dribbling.

Frank Timmerman and Lee Douglas, two men in the Hawks' front office, saw Golden. Both were impressed.

They said to me, "Why don't you have him come and do some ball-handling tricks during time outs?"

After that, we'd drive up from Barnesville to Atlanta on game nights, and Golden would entertain the crowd during time outs. Tony was 22 months old at the time, and I incorporated him into the act too. They'd do a one-ball dribble, then a two-ball routine. Then I brought out a Dr. J mini-goal and they'd play one-on-one.

The crowd loved it, and soon Frank suggested that we put together an eight-minute halftime show.

And so we did. I brought in Eliott, Sunshine and Israel so our entire family could get involved. They'd all practice an assortment of ballhandling drills together.

It was really a fun and cute thing because they were all so young. Each of my five kids could dribble three regular-sized basketballs, at the same time, down the entire length of the court and back. Eliott, my oldest son, could do quite well dribbling four basketballs at once.

We came up with a name for the act: the Little Nuggets. My nickname as a player was "Little Nugget," since I was 5-foot-10 and 100 pounds.

During the summer months, the Little Nuggets would come with me to the basketball camps I worked at. They'd demonstrate some dribbling, and then I'd give a lecture.

A lot of what I talked about in those lectures was the importance of sticking together as families. I remember reading an article about Bill Cosby in the newspaper back then; he was touring the United States to raise awareness about the lack of fathers among the minority population. In the 1980's, 25 percent of black kids in America grew up without a man in the home. Here we are a quarter-century later, and it's almost triple that.

I think that's a tragedy. We need good and strong families in our society, and I've always tried to coach and preach the importance of family.

Practicing and preparing our routine gave us a lot of time together, and we spent a lot of time on the road. As our reputation grew, the Little

Nuggets traveled to perform all over the South. We performed halftime shows at Florida State, Georgia Tech, Alabama, Mississippi State. We did our act at an Auburn-Kentucky SEC game.

When Israel was still in diapers, we had a performance out at Auburn.

He had little knobby knees, and he'd run out on the court and dribble a basketball. It was the most adorable thing in the world.

We had the entire performance choreographed. I had music playing over the P.A. system to accompany us, and when a song ended I knew to get to the next part of the show. But when a particular song ended and I turned to Israel to give him a ball to dribble, he was sound asleep on the court.

I'd made a simple miscalculation. Auburn is on Central time, and I'd forgotten to make the adjustment. It might have been 9:30 p.m. in Georgia, but it was 8:30 p.m. in Alabama. The crowd was in stitches, seeing that little guy just dozing off on the floor like that. I had to wake him up, and he took a swing at me! It was bedtime, and he was going to get his sleep, whether 10,000 people were watching or not.

The kids loved it when we got to travel. The Little Nuggets were invited to NBA games around the country. When we went to do our act at a Washington Bullets game, there was a limousine to pick us up. We traveled to Milwaukee and performed at the first McDonald's Open, an event at which NBA teams played against squads from other countries.

We got autographed basketballs from the Bulls and Cavaliers when we performed in Chicago and Cleveland. The largest crowd we performed for was 33,000 people, at a Detroit Pistons game. The kids got to meet Isaiah Thomas and Bill Laimbeer in the locker room afterwards.

The Little Nuggets were ranked as one of the top NBA halftime shows in the 1980's, and we performed for over 400,000 people if you add the game crowds and the camps together.

Our family received a lot of positive press. There were a lot of articles written about us in newspapers all around the South. We were seen on TBS, NBC, CBS and George Michael's Sports Machine. CNN even did a piece on us once.

But that was all secondary to me. The most important thing, as far as I was concerned, was that I was able to invest time in my children. When

I came home from a long day at Gordon College, I'd be dead tired from teaching and coaching all day. My kids would all come up to me at the door yelling, "Daddy! Daddy!" They'd be so excited to shoot ball with me, or put a new wrinkle into our Little Nuggets act.

I've always felt that it is a father's responsibility to teach his children what he knows, and that being tired should never enter into it. So we had an agreement: any time they asked me to shoot baskets, I'd always go. (Sometimes I wouldn't go *right then*, but we would always go play before the night was over.)

I remember many nights when we would go to the gym at 11:30 at night, and practice until one or two o'clock in the morning. They were all still so little then that none of them had school the next day.

I couldn't believe how much Golden in particular loved to shoot the ball. I remember one day, I took him to the gym at 6 o'clock in the evening and I said to myself, "I'm going to see how long this little guy lasts."

At 3 a.m., I finally said, "Son, I'm going home to bed."

I was convinced that as long as I rebounded for him, no matter how many hours in a row, he would be shooting. I don't know if there's a place in the Guinness Book of World Records for that sort of thing, but Golden would be in there if given the opportunity.

One time, Golden, Israel, Tony and I got up at four o'clock in the morning. We left the house at about five o'clock, and drove to Franklin Springs, Georgia for a 9:30 a.m. performance at a summer basketball camp. Then we drove down to Florida State in Tallahassee to do a half-time show at 1:30. We got back in the car and drove back north to Waleska, Georgia in time for a 9 p.m. performance at Reinhardt College.

When we got back home at around midnight, I stopped and thought, "Oh my goodness, what have I done?" I had a five-year-old, a four-year-old and a three-year-old who had all been on the court for over four hours. We'd been in the car all day long.

— — — — —

I was never trying to exploit my family. I saw the Little Nuggets as an opportunity to play a lot of basketball with my five children. They all grew up, and it happened too fast, but I'm so grateful that I was able to spend so much time with them when they were kids. There were so many fond memories that I'll never forget.

The act never made us rich. There were seven people relying on that $23,000 that Gordon College gave me for coaching and teaching. And that was gross; taxes took a third of that.

My friend Terry Lenahan lived in Atlanta, and he had season tickets to all 41 home Atlanta Hawks games. He'd go to about half of those games, and he'd give the rest to me. I'd go to see the Hawks play occasionally, but more often than not I'd make the hour-long drive up to Atlanta to scalp those seats outside the Omni.

I did that so I could get $20, so I could buy groceries for my family. I'd spend a fiver on gas, but I'd end up clearing $15. I don't think Terry ever knew that our family would never have made it without his Hawks tickets.

I was on the advisory board of the Atlanta Tip Off Club, and I helped organize promotions for them. One of my assignments was to make sure the coaching clinics ran smoothly.

One time, there was a clinic in Atlanta where then-Pepperdine head coach Jim Harrick and the legendary Lute Olson from Arizona were speaking. I left Barnesville with a quarter-tank of gas (just enough to get to the city and back) and $1.83 in my pocket. I used a quarter to call Terry and ask him if I could stay at his house for two nights, and sleep on his rollaway bed. Then I was left with $1.58.

As I was setting up the clinic at the hotel on Friday afternoon, I noticed that there was a football clinic finishing up in the ballroom adjacent to ours. As the hotel workers were cleaning up the football room after a banquet, I went in and grabbed a couple of turkey croissant sandwiches off a table. I wrapped them up in some plastic, took them back to a custodians' closet, and put them underneath a bucket on a high shelf. I flipped the bucket upside down, because I didn't want any rats coming along and eating my food.

I was lucky because Jackie Bradford, the executive director of the Naismith Awards, took me out to eat that night. We had mesquite quail at a really nice restaurant. I was hoping that some coaches could smell my breath when we got back!

On Saturday morning, there was a continental breakfast, so I was taken care of food-wise. But that afternoon, once all the coaches broke for lunch, I went into the janitor's closet to retrieve my turkey sandwiches.

There was a big problem, though. Jackie asked me to take Lute Olson to the airport on Sunday afternoon.

I met the famous coach, and we hit it off well. I found out he had five kids, just like I did. But by driving those extra few miles, my gas tank was emptied out. I knew I wasn't going to be able to make it home to Barnesville, because I was down to my last eight cents. I'd called Jeanne six times that weekend on the pay phone.

Fifteen miles away from Barnesville, I was on empty. I pulled into a service station on Interstate 75, and told the clerk behind the counter that I needed some gas to get home. I explained that I didn't have any money, but that I was the head men's basketball coach at Gordon College.

"Do you have any proof of that?" he asked me.

I had a stack of Atlanta Pro Basketball Camp brochures in my glove compartment, so I went and retrieved one to show him. On the front of the brochure, there were pictures of Mike Fratello, Bob Reinhart, and Tony Ingle.

"Here I am," I said. He looked at the picture, looked at me, then gave me five dollars' worth of gas.

So I was able to make it back to Barnesville that night. The next day, I drove back up to the service station and gave that clerk his money back.

Jeanne and I rented a farm house in Barnesville, a few miles from Gordon's campus. Our landlord owned 115 acres of land, and there were only two houses on that parcel. It was an old country-style house with 12-foot ceilings, lots of drafts, and plenty of holes for field mice to come inside.

But we were so poor the rats lost weight. I used to tell a joke that my son once opened up the refrigerator in front of company and I whipped him. "Don't do that, son, you'll make them think we've got food!"

That house was a constant adventure. In addition to the mice, we had leaky pipes. The toilet water was always frozen. The "PM Magazine" TV show came over to do a story on the Little Nuggets, and the nice lady interviewer stepped in a big pile of crawling ants.

Once, our finances were so bad that I couldn't feed my family. We'd sold every piece of furniture that was worth anything.

We owned a color television set that I'd purchased for $95 at a "smoke sale" after a hotel fire. The only way we could pick up the Atlanta stations was to attach a clothes hanger and a big ball of aluminum foil. But it was the only item of value we had left, and I had to sell it if we were going to eat.

I remember loading that TV into our car, so I could take it down to the pawn shop. As I came out of our long driveway, I glanced in my rear view mirror and I saw my wife and children together on the porch, watching me as I drove away. My eyes filled with tears when I saw them all standing there, so unhappy.

What I was doing wasn't fair to Jeanne or the kids, I thought. I was chasing this pie-in-the-sky dream of becoming a national championship coach. In the process, I was hurting the people I loved so much. They deserved a better daddy and a stronger provider.

Tears rolled down my face, and I was beating the steering wheel with both hands. "This is crazy, this is crazy," I kept saying over and over.

As I drove towards the pawn shop, I vowed that I would quit coaching when the season was over. Things couldn't get any worse. Because of my selfishness, our kids didn't even have a TV to watch.

I negotiated a price of $50 for that television set. When I came back home, my wife and kids loaded up in the wagon and we drove down to the grocery store. God bless Jeanne, she really knew how to stretch money back then. She bought rice and franks and beans and potatoes, and we came back home with enough to feed the whole family for weeks.

The children and I went to the gym to practice some Little Nuggets routines. I helped them study, then we played some family games, and I prayed with them before bed.

I hid the tears well, and it was like any other night in the Ingle household. Except, of course, for the empty table where the TV had been.

When the season was over, I told Jeanne that I was going to quit coaching. I said that I would find a better job so I could be a better provider.

She looked me dead in the eye.

"Oh, *no* you don't," she said. "Don't you *ever* give up on your dream, Tony. You've come too far, and you've beaten a lot of odds to get to where you are. We are going to make it as a family, and you are going to make it as a coach."

As Zig Ziglar (my hero in the world of motivational speaking) might say, Jeanne gave me a "check up from the neck up" that night.

She offered to go out and get a job to help bring in some income, but I couldn't let her. She had her hands full raising our five children, and I remembered how hard my mom worked in the carpet mills, how it had worn her down. I couldn't bear the idea of Jeanne going through that.

We had to do without the amenities of modern life, but we always had the old-fashioned love that unites a husband and wife.

— — — — — —

Money was tight at Gordon College, too. I remember that Hugh Durham, head coach at the University of Georgia, sent some basketball schedules with some rubber bands around them. I called him up and asked him if he could send some more.

"Hey, could you send me some more schedules?" I asked.

"Why, are you going to come bring your team?" Coach Durham replied.

"No, Coach, we need more *rubber bands*," I said. "We're on a tight budget over here!"

I signed 13 players in my first year at Gordon, but there were five young men who came to the first practice late. I made them run laps. The next day, they came to practice late, and I ran them again. And I told them that if they were late again, they'd be off the team.

The next day, as I was walking past the student center on my way to practice, I saw those five guys in there shooting pool. So I barred the door to the locker room, and when they came in - late again - I confronted them.

"Gentlemen," I said. "I told you twice. If you're going to play for me, you're going to be on time."

I let all five of them go that day. That left me with eight players. I lost some talent, that's for sure, but I wanted to make sure that everybody knew that we were laying a good, solid foundation at Gordon College. We were going to build a program that people could be proud of.

There were some interesting moments. In the second half of a game at Emmanuel College, the referee blew his whistle against one of my players, and I disagreed with the call. I grabbed my coat and threw it.

I'd forgotten that the team's meal money was in the coat, and cash came flying out all over the court.

The official blew the whistle again to call a technical foul on me. I was on the floor scooping up the money, my players were all down there helping me pick it up, and all the while I was arguing with the referee. Then he blew his whistle again, and kicked me out of the game.

I had no assistant coach, and only eight ballplayers. So as I was leaving the court, I turned to Jeff Manley and said, "You're the captain of the team. Now you're the coach too."

Jeff was sitting on the bench at the time, so his first order of business was subbing himself into the game!

There was a great junior college coach in south Georgia named Brian Crowder. Before a game, he came down the sideline to shake my hand.

Unbeknownst to me, he had a little buzzer in his hand. When he shook my hand, he shocked me! It kind of ticked me off.

Coach Crowder had a good team that was ranked 16th in the nation. "Coach, I want you to know I'm going to vote for you for Coach of the Year," I told him. "But only if you don't beat us bad. I'll tell you what... if you beat us by less than 25, I'll vote for you." That got his attention.

"You're serious?" he asked me, his eyes getting big. "Don't you be kidding with me now, Tony."

"Nope, I'm dead serious," I replied. "I know you're gonna beat us, but only beat us by 15 or 20. If you beat us real bad, my feelings will be so hurt that I'm simply going to forget to vote for you."

We ended up winning the game, 105-88. I looked over at Coach Crowder, and I could tell he was mad.

I wasn't interested in any personal trophies, I wanted the national championship. In my second year at Gordon, we were invited to play at a tournament in Nashville hosted by San Aquinas Junior College. They told me that we'd have to play Vincennes of Indiana.

"Have to?" I replied. "I *want* to."

I definitely wanted a shot at the team that played for the national title the previous year. Vincennes is arguably the most legendary two-year program in the United States, and they won the national tournament in Hutchinson, Kansas when I played in junior college. I wanted to build the kind of program that could eventually beat teams like Vincennes. I wanted to take Gordon College all the way to the finals at Hutch.

We had a two-point lead over Vincennes with two minutes left to play. I don't know if the fact that Vincennes stayed at the Nashville Marriottt, with three square meals a day, had anything to do with them coming back to win that game. I had to wake up at 5 o'clock in the morning on game day and fetch my players some Little Debbie Swiss Rolls, milk and orange juice.

But I do know that legendary coach Don Meyer, who was at Lipscomb College at the time and would later become the NCAA's all-time winningest coach with over 900 victories, came up to me afterwards. Coach Meyer praised me for some of the X's and O's I put into the game. Our little talk that day did wonders for my self-confidence as a coach.

I also remember that our bus heater went out on our drive back to Barnesville. I was walking like Chuck Connors for two weeks, bowlegged and frozen that way.

Gordon went 18-11 in my first year. Then we won 21 games each in my second and third seasons. We made the state playoffs all three years. But it was in that third season, in 1988, when I knew we had become good enough to take a shot at the national title.

The first time we played Brewton Parker that season, we fell into a huge early hole. When the other team went into the locker room for halftime, I ordered my players to stay out on the floor and practice until the second half started.

We came back from 25 points down to win that game.

Gordon had to play Brewton Parker again for the regional championship, the prize being a trip to Hutchinson and the national tournament. Our rematch was a tough, hard-fought game.

We held on to a one-point lead with 33 seconds remaining. Chuck Johnson, the best foul shooter in the whole state of Georgia, was on the line. Chuck missed the front end of a one-and-one, and in his valiant attempt to grab the rebound, committed a foul.

The clock stopped. Brewton Parker went to the foul line, and they made both shots to take a one-point lead. With 18 seconds left, we had to go the length of the floor. We picked our shot well (an eight-foot jumper), but it rolled in and out. Brewton Parker rebounded, we fouled, they made the foul shots, and our season was over.

I'd lost a lot of ballgames, but I can't remember a loss hurting so badly. Afterwards, Jeanne and I agreed it would be best that she take the kids back to her mother's house in Dalton for a while. I needed to absorb the loss and let the pain be healed by time. I don't remember speaking a single word as I drove the bus back to Barnesville.

I settled into our old country house, all alone, waiting for the hurt to go away. But the next morning, I received a phone call.

It was my old friend Bobby Cremins from Georgia Tech on the line.

Previous: The U.S. patented drag shot for the North Whitfield High School Pioneers.

Above: In a hotel room in Hutchinson, Kansas, the night of my NJCAA tournament injury.

Right (top to bottom): with teammates at the Dalton J.C. banquet; Me, Bobby Cremins and Bob Reinhart.

Above: I can sing with the best of them! Yelling at players, not officials.
Right: The cartwheel play at Cherokee High. Oh, yes we did!

Top: The Little Nuggets! Eliott, Sunshine, Golden, Tony Jr., and Israel.

Right (top to bottom): A newspaper clipping from back in Georgia after I took the interim head coaching job at BYU; collector's items from my brief and storied stand-up career.

Next page, left: two of the many people who thought I should have been given a chance after the 0-19 season.

Next page, right: me and TNT studio host Ernie Johnson.

Ingle: BYU now 'my program'

By Norman Arey
STAFF WRITER

Tony Ingle was recruiting in Louisiana and looking forward to a trip to his native Georgia. At 5:45 p.m. Tuesday, the telephone rang and changed his life.

Before the call, Ingle was a Brigham Young assistant coach who had bounced around several states in pursuit of a dream. When he answered the phone, that dream come true. Roger Reid had been fired at BYU, and Ingle had been named interim head coach.

Ingle

Dad's team: Tony Ingle and basketball-playing kids (from left) Tony Jr., Eliott, Israel, Sunshine and Golden in 1988.

"When I converted to the Mormon religion, Budweiser laid off their second shift," Ingle said.

The couple has five children who later became known as the Little Nuggets — a juvenile edition of the Harlem Globetrotters. Eliott, Sunshine, Golden, Tony Jr. and Israel performed at halftime at high school, college and NBA games. They were once voted one of the top halftime shows in the NBA.

Wednesday, Ingle realized there was work to be done before Saturday's game.

"Michael Jackson needs a stage, Flipper needs water, and all I need is a chance," Ingle said. "We lost two starters to injury and another one left for personal reasons. It's like running Daytona with two tires off. I need to get out and recruit. I've never seen a jockey carry his horse around

Presents

An Evening with
Tony Ingle
September 17, 2002
8:00 pm

Located 177 W 300 S Provo, UT

www.johnnybscomedyclub.com

Presents

An Evening with
Tony Ingle
September 17, 2002
8:00 pm

Located 177 W 300 S Provo, UT

www.johnnybscomedyclub.com

Tony T's

Kenney Wilkinson, left, and his daughter Summer, of Wilkinson Trophy show off their Tony Ingle T-shirts. Summer designed the shirts to gain support for BYU interim basketball coach Tony Ingle. Anybody seen any Ken Wagner hats or Dick Hunsaker sweatshirts around town?

Above: I was founder and executive director of the John & Nellie Wooden Awards for five years. Here I am with the great Wizard of Westwood himself.

Right (top to bottom): Cutting down the nets after winning a Peach Belt title at Kennesaw; 2004 Division II national champions!

Next page, left (top to bottom): Kennesaw State goes Division I; me and the "Stormin' Mormon" himself, former BYU and NBA star Shawn Bradley.

Next page, right: National recognition at Kennesaw.

Tony Ingle has Kennesaw rolling, despite a weird beverage vice.

Love Potion

How is a D-I newbie leading the Atlantic Sun? Kyle Whelliston found out that the secret to Kennesaw State's shocking conference start is lots of love ... and cherry juice-flavored Slim-Fast. **Story**

- The Mid Life: 10 hours of HBCU hoops | Wrap: Steve Lavin
- Illinois-Indiana (ESPN, 7 ET) | SHU-Villanova (ESPN Classic, 7:30)

Above: Family. Front row, left to right: Tony Jr., Eliott, Sunshine and Israel. Back row: Golden, me, and Jeanne.

5
KEEPING THE FAITH

BACK WHEN I WAS AT CHEROKEE HIGH SCHOOL, I HAD applied for the job at the Division II University of Alabama-Huntsville. Out of 202 applicants, I made it to the top seven.

But UAH was only going to bring in three applicants for interviews. I did the gracious thing and wrote a letter to Paul Brand, the athletic director there. I congratulated him on the hire, and I asked him what I needed to do in case the job ever opened up again in the future.

Paul wrote me a very kind letter. He let me know that I was a very serious candidate, but that I didn't have any college coaching experience.

Three years later, in 1989, I was at Gordon College. Brian Crowder (the guy with the hand-buzzer) told me that the UAH job was open again. I sent in my updated résumé, and then I forgot all about it. I was busy coaching the Generals to the Georgia state junior college championship.

The morning after we lost by one point to Brewton Parker in the regional championship game, I was as low as the dry part of a whale turd.

And that's when Bobby Cremins called me.

"Someone on the Alabama-Huntsville hiring committee called me and asked me about you," he said. "Get on it, Tony!"

That snapped me out of my misery. I had some of my coaching friends call Paul Brand to lobby for my cause. I pulled out all the stops. I had Mike Fratello, Hubie Brown, and Bobby make some calls. That Wednesday, I got the word that I was in the top three, and that I'd earned an interview date the following week.

But something happened in the interim. I became sick as a dog.

God drove that car to Huntsville; I don't know how I made it. I had to take naps at rest areas, and a couple of times I had to stop and puke out of the driver's side window of the car. I tried to call members on the committee to let them know I'd be late. I ended up in Huntsville nearly three hours after my originally scheduled interview time had passed.

There was a hotel on campus, and Paul came and picked me up after I had checked in. "Let's go out to eat," he said. "I have a taste for a minestrone soup and a salad at the Olive Garden. Now how does that sound to you?"

Eating was the last thing I wanted to do. "That sounds perfect," I managed.

(What I was really thinking at the time was, "I'll just eat and puke, and then I'll be on my way, thank you very much.")

"Tony, you and I both know you applied for this job three years ago," he asked me in the car. "Now, why would you apply for it three years later?"

"Mr. Brand," I replied. "Three years ago, you sent me a letter letting me know I was in the top seven. That really meant a lot to me. I asked you what I needed to do, and you told me that I had to be a head coach in college. I followed your advice, and I now have three years of college coaching experience. But you made a mistake by not hiring me the last time, and I don't want you to make the same mistake again."

The next day, I interviewed in front of the whole committee. Afterwards, a local reporter asked Paul Brand how the process had gone.

"Let's just put it this way," the A.D. said to the reporter. "I just spent two and a half glorious hours with the Will Rogers of basketball."

The day I got the job at UAH, Jeanne and the kids moved out to Huntsville to join me. I was an NCAA Division II head coach! I had gone from $23,000 at Gordon to $29,000 in my new position.

And compared to Gordon College, Huntsville was the Taj Mahal. UAH had a full weight room, a study hall, and a full staff of assistants and marketing people to help me. Instead of doing it all myself, I was finally in a position to delegate.

The reason the job had opened up in the first place was because Alabama-Huntsville had gone 4-24 the previous year. The team won just 16 games in three years, so we had to bring some respectability back to the program. I was able to sign all the players I wanted. I hired a bright young assistant named Lenny Acuff, who was ready for the challenge.

We had some interesting games that season. Thomas Jones scored 55 points against Lane College, and I took him out of the game with five minutes to play. I simply lost track of his output. But he was such a fine selfless player and a great teammate that he never complained about it.

If I'd been aware of how many points he had, I would have left Thomas in to see if he could score 60. That would have been a nice round number, which would have brought our university and team some national recognition. That's part of how Division II works; you get attention any way you can.

In an echo of my days at Southeast High School and Gordon College, Alabama-Huntsville was an independent school that was not in a regular conference. We had to work hard to get on other teams' schedules, and it seemed that the only schools that wanted to play us were powerhouses that wanted to give us the beatings of our lives. Our only path to the NCAA Division II Tournament was to somehow get an at-large bid. For D-II independents like UAH, that was harder than jumping over Snake River Canyon on a unicycle.

I never complained, though, not for one second.

Our final game of the year was at home against Delta State from Mississippi. We went into that matchup with a 9-18 record. They'd beaten us by 41 points in our first meeting at their place, and the only thing positive about that first game was that none of our players were injured. Delta was easily the best team we'd played all year, and they were just using us as a tuneup for the playoffs.

But we chose to stay positive. Before the rematch, I had my team practice a full-court out-of-bounds play designed to be used in the final seconds of a close ballgame.

And it just so happened that we played our best ball of the year that night. We held that great Delta State team close all game long, and we were tied with eight seconds remaining. We inbounded the ball under our own basket with the length of the floor to go.

I called for our team to run our new play. I turned to my assistant Lenny Acuff and said, "Let's see if we can coach."

We ran the play to perfection, and good ol' Thomas Jones scored at the buzzer to win the game for UAH. Our bench players ran onto the floor and mobbed Thomas, and they were all jumping up and down and laughing. This victory got us headed in the right direction.

It was if we had just won the NBA Finals, not our tenth game in 28 tries.

———————

One of my summer activities during those early college coaching years was going out to Utah to help with the basketball camps at Brigham Young University. That's where I met Roger Reid, who was a BYU assistant at the time.

Roger was one of the most interesting people I ever met. He was a phenomenal athlete growing up, and he played professional baseball in the White Sox and Braves organizations. He was a tireless and ambitious worker, too. In 1978, he jumped from a high school job in Clearfield, Utah straight to an assistant position at BYU. He had served there for over a decade.

I also knew Roger as a very committed family man, and that's why he was such an inspiration to me. I remember one night while I was out in Utah working a camp; Roger invited me over to his house to meet his wife and kids.

He once told me that a father should never be so tired that he couldn't be there for his children. That's why I made sure I shot baskets with my kids whenever they wanted to. Roger had a baby who died suddenly in his sleep, and he talked about how hard that was on him and his wife. It just tore me up to hear those stories.

Roger and I became very good friends. One summer I drove up to Idaho with him, and we worked camps together from 8 a.m. to 10 p.m. All day long, just me and him. One time, I threw out my back and I had to perform my duties from a chair while he ran around at double-speed. We made a great team. During my time at Gordon College and UAH, Roger and I would always write each other letters and check up on each other's teams.

In the spring of 1989, BYU fired head coach Ladell Anderson. I remember watching the NCAA Tournament on CBS that year, and Brent Musberger said during the broadcast, "Longtime assistant Roger Reid has just been named the head coach at Brigham Young University."

It was March 20. Roger called me that very night. "Tony, you're at the top of my list," he said.

"Wow, I'm going to be an assistant coach at BYU," I said to myself after I hung up the phone.

—————

The opportunity at BYU was very meaningful for me. I joined the Church of Jesus Christ of Latter Day Saints in 1976.

I always wanted to go to church growing up. I always felt like it might have helped me figure things out. To me, it was logical that if a person with physical problems went to a hospital, somebody with spiritual weaknesses or wounds would go to church.

But my family and I never went.

Jeanne was always a member of the Mormon Church, and I knew the moment I met her that she was a good person. She was raised right, with solid morals and values. One day while we were dating, some missionaries came over to her house.

"There's something about you," one of them said to me.

"Oh no, I'm being set up," I said to myself. "They're after my soul.

Don't let 'em get you, Tony, *run for it!*"

The missionaries gave me a copy of the Book of Mormon, and challenged me to read some of it and to pray. When we met again at Jeanne's house later on that week, they asked me if I'd read it.

I replied that I had. I'd gone ahead and read a few verses, and even found it mildly interesting.

"Mr. Ingle, did you pray?" one of the missionaries asked me.

I didn't really believe in God. Besides, I drank, I cussed, and I had all these personality problems. I knew I was a sinner.

In fact, I didn't even know *how* to pray at that time. This is how bad it was: I was the vice-president of my senior class in high school, and I had to lead a prayer at our high school graduation. Deborah Sloan had to write a prayer for me on an index card so that I could read it out loud.

But I nodded sheepishly. I loved Jeanne, so I'd given it a try. I remember being so embarrassed, looking over at her. She was smiling from ear to ear.

"How did it make you feel?" the missionary asked.

"To be honest with you, I didn't feel anything," I replied. "I don't think I did it right."

"When we pray, here's what we do," he said, smiling. "First, we get on our knees. It's said that a man stands tallest when he's on his knees praying.

Then we address Heavenly Father. It's as if we're picking up the phone, and we're directing the call to Him. We thank Him for things that we're thankful for, and we ask Him for what we're asking for. Then we close in the name of Jesus Christ."

"But when you offer that prayer," he continued. "Listen to your spirit. Feel your spirit. Some people call it a burning sensation inside, some call it a comfort. But that's your spirit. The more you pray, the better you'll get at it. It's just like anything else that you practice to get good at." That made a little more sense to me. But when should I do it?

"Pray in the morning," he said. "You can also pray with your eyes open... you can talk to God as you're going through your day. Then at night, kneel back down and give accountability for how you did that day."

"*Man,*" I exclaimed. "Y'all pray three times a day? Not just at night, like 'Now I lay me down to sleep?'"

"Oh no, no, Mr. Ingle," he explained. "We don't sleep in fear. We live in faith."

I decided right then to join the Mormon Church. I took the Discussions, and I was baptized.

In the Doctrine and Covenants, there's something called the Word of Wisdom which says that we should abstain from alcohol and tobacco.

The idea is that our bodies are tabernacles, and that we should take care of them.

Soon after I joined the Church, Budweiser laid off the third shift.

But as I got better at prayer, I learned that the greatest power is the power of God. I wanted to tap into that power. And I knew that as a young coach, my job was to build people up. First, I had to build my own character. I knew I had to be up before I could lift others up.

One of the things I've done wherever I've coached is put this quote over the chalkboard: "Seek Ye First The Kingdom of Heaven." I don't really talk about heaven a lot, I don't preach it or teach it to my players at all.

But I do let the players see that quote, and they can decide for themselves. I really believe that if we're seeking the Lord before we seek anything else, then we definitely have our priorities straight.

It's been said that families that pray together stay together, and I also believe that basketball teams that pray together stay together too. When I was in college, we always had a prayer before games, and I still try to pray with my teams. Just a small little prayer thanking Heavenly Father for our blessings and asking for His spirit to be with us. I know that the other teams are praying in their locker rooms as well, but I still feel like it's an important thing to do.

— — — — — —

Three months after Roger was promoted to head coach, BYU hired me as the top assistant. For the second time in as many years, our family was on the move again.

But this time, we were going to live in a comfortable house. Our financial struggles seemed to be finally over. I was in Division I now!

I'll never forget my first day as a D-I assistant coach. I was escorted to the Smith Field House to receive some clothes with the BYU Cougars logo on them, to wear during recruiting trips. Floyd "Mr. J" Johnson, the school's longtime equipment manager, had me sit on a table with my feet dangling off the edge. He asked me what size shoe I wore.

"If they're free, I take anything from a 5 to a 13," I replied.

Mr. J grabbed the back heel of my right shoe. And there was my big toe, sticking out of my old socks.

"*Wow!*" someone shouted. "I don't know whether to shoot it or feed it!"

So I got a box full of brand new socks. Mr. J took pity on me, and gave me some extra BYU logo items, like tees and polo shirts. He even threw in a new pair of shoes. I was so happy to get free clothes, I walked out of the fieldhouse like a drum major in the Grambling marching band.

My introduction to the Cougar fans came during a hour-long coaches' show on local TV. A lot of people don't realize how basketball-crazy Utah really is; this program was one of the highest-rated shows in the state.

Coach Reid was there on the set. Charles Bradley was there, he was a first-round draft pick for the Boston Celtics who played his college ball at Wyoming, and now he was an assistant at BYU. And in the corner, there was little Tony Ingle from Huntingdon College.

Roger got most of the attention, of course. People wanted to hear how he planned to bring the program back to the NCAA Tournament. A lot of people remembered Charles from when he played in the Western Athletic Conference. Charles and BYU legend Danny Ainge had some great wars back in the day, and folks were eager to call up and share those memories.

I sat there all night, not getting any questions. Not until the very end of the show, when a nice little old lady took pity on me. She called up and said, "If you wouldn't mind, I would like to address a question to Coach Ingle."

The camera zoomed in on me. The little red light came on. And that's when I realized that there were probably people at home lying in bed watching TV, or sitting in their lounge chairs after a long day at work, and they were about to get a good look at me and my face for the first time.

"I think that's a great question," I said. "But before I answer, I would like to remind our viewers of something. Please do not adjust your tracking... I *really do* look like this."

That single line is what most viewers remembered about the show. I heard references to the TV tracking knob for years after that.

In my second game as an assistant coach under Roger, we were playing at Penn State. the Nittany Lions had taken 47 foul shots in that game. With a few seconds remaining, our star player Andy Toolson was fouled, and he shot a one-and-one. If he had made the first one to earn the second shot, it would be only the eighth foul shot for BYU.

I expressed my displeasure about the disparity to an official.

"Hey, sir," I called out. He didn't turn around to look at me.

I tried again. "Mr. Referee, can I ask you a question?"

That's when he turned to me. "I don't talk to assistant coaches," he said dismissively.

"I have been a head coach for 13 years," I told him. "This is my second game as a college assistant here at Brigham Young University. And you know that we're all Mormons here. I'm not going to use any profanity with you. I'm just somewhat confused at this juncture, and would certainly appreciate the opportunity to ask you a personal question."

He walked towards the BYU bench, folded his arms, and looked me squarely in the eye. "OK, Coach," he said. "What's your question?" "Sir," I inquired. "Are you using a flathead or a Phillips?" He got the message. Lucky for me, it also got him laughing.

On a cold December night with about a foot of snow on the ground, we played a home game against Siena University. We had a great crowd that night, about 18,000 people made it out to the arena. I was visiting on the sidelines with Saints head coach Mike Deane before the ballgame, watching warmups.

"Hey, Coach Ingle," he said. "You Mormons abstain from drugs and alcohol, right?"

"Sure do," I replied proudly.

"Well, then I can honestly say that I've never seen so many good livers in one place in all my life," he deadpanned, scanning the huge crowd.

Coach Deane told me that he had brought the team in from upstate New York the night before. He set a midnight curfew for his players. All lights had to be out, no exceptions, because playing BYU was not going to be an easy task. The team needed its sleep.

One of his captains raised his hand and asked, "Hey Coach, we're in Provo, Utah and there's no nightlife here. Can we have curfew at 10 o'clock instead?"

That may have been the first time in Division I history a team asked for an earlier curfew!

I loved living in Orem. It was heaven on earth for a Mormon like me. My kids loved it too, and they had so much fun growing up there. When we held practices, I'd bring my sons over to hang out and watch TV in my office.

One day, we'd been going for hours, and our coaching staff was really working the players hard. Roger was wearing out his whistle. We had them doing non-stop defensive drills and wind sprints and half-court games all day.

Then, all of a sudden, a Domino's Pizza man came walking across the floor. "Are you Tony Ingle?" he asked.

I was embarrassed. I thought I had been the victim of a practical joke or something. Here we were in the middle of a serious Division I basketball practice, and here comes this guy delivering a pizza.

The smell of that hot, fresh pie was wafting throughout the entire building. The players were dripping with sweat, looking at that red and blue box all bug-eyed. Their tongues were hanging out. They hadn't eaten anything in hours.

Then all of a sudden, out of the corner of my eye, there was my nine-year-old son, Tony Ingle Jr., hiding in the corner holding a twenty-dollar bill in his hand. "Hey, that's our pizza!" he called out.

And that was the end of practice for the day. We all had to eat!

— — — — — —

Success came quickly for the new coaching staff at BYU. In the months after I was hired, we recruited Shawn "The Stormin' Mormon" Bradley – all 7-foot-6 of him. Shawn was one of the best high school players in America, and he had narrowed his field down to Duke, UCLA, Utah and BYU.

One day, Roger, Charles and I arrived at Shawn's home in Castle Dale, Utah. I was sporting a brand new $600 suit from the Mr. Mac Clothing Store, and I'd never felt so dapper in my life. We got out of the car and made our way to the porch, and all of a sudden a giant Saint Bernard came running up to me and put its two huge dirty paws on my nice new suit...

just as Mrs. Theresa Bradley opened the front door.

I specifically remember how tall everybody in the Bradley family was. His dad was 6-foot-8 and his mom was 6-foot-1. Shawn's younger brother was 6-foot-10.

The visit went wonderfully. I also had the wonderful opportunity to sample Mrs. Bradley's homemade desserts. They should be marketed nationwide, so all of America might be able to enjoy them.

The next day, Coach Reid received a call from Shawn. Shawn was tired of the long, drawn-out recruiting process, and he felt strongly that BYU was where he should attend school.

It was a major recruiting victory for the three of us. We jumped up and down, laughing and hugging. We celebrated in the great Mormon tradition – by ordering a round of milkshakes.

We inked Shawn to a letter of intent in the fall. In our coaching staff's first year, BYU went 21-9 and made the 1990 NCAA Tournament as an at-large team out of the WAC. We were a No. 12 seed, and lost by two points by Clemson in the first round.

The next year, we got Shawn in as a freshman, and the whole town of Provo went crazy over him. Heck, the whole country went nuts for Shawn.

We played at the New York City Holiday Festival at Madison Square Garden in a field that included Rutgers, USC and Maryland. Shawn was treated like a rock star. People wanted to get their picture taken with him, and everybody wanted his autograph. The media was always chasing after Shawn, trying to ask him questions.

I remember how gracefully he accepted all the attention throughout his entire career at BYU. He averaged nearly 15 points and eight rebounds per game as a freshman. With Shawn, we won the 1991 WAC championship with a 20-13 record and went to the Big Dance as a No. 10 seed. That's where we beat Virginia in an upset, before a very good Arizona team ended our season. That was Shawn's only year with us; he left and went on his mission, then became the second overall draft pick by the Philadelphia 76ers a couple of years later.

Shawn was probably the most interesting young man I have ever coached. Some of the other players resented him for all the publicity he was getting, and some didn't like how he would stay by himself a lot and not mix and mingle with his teammates.

It wasn't that he was stuck-up or arrogant. He was at times a very shy and quiet kid. Shawn carried a huge burden on his shoulders every time we went on the court, and some of our fans placed unrealistic expectations on him. There were those who thought that because he was 7-foot-6, there was no excuse if he didn't score every time he shot the ball.

I tried to place myself in Shawn's gigantic shoes. What would I feel like if everybody asked me to be perfect, and then get better from there? What if I was the one expected to win every game for my team, night in and night out? I fully understood why Shawn left early and took the available option of a $43 million NBA contract. If you're going to be sec-ondguessed and cursed at all the time, you might as well get paid for it.

We played in five NCAA Tournaments and one NIT during my time at BYU. But as the 1990's continued along, I started to get the feeling that our run was destined to end.

We lost our recruiting momentum. Matt Christensen was a 6-10 cen-ter and an LDS member from Massachusetts. One night, I was visiting with him at his hotel and I knew that Mike Krzyzewski from Duke was outside waiting in his car. It was late at night, and I took as long as I could. I foolishly thought that if I waited long enough, Coach K would get tired and drive away.

I remember peeping out of the hotel window just before midnight. There he was, sitting in his car, waiting his turn.

Finally, Matt said to me, "Coach Ingle, I'm not trying to be rude, but Coach K has been waiting for quite some time. Shouldn't we wrap things up?"

That's when I knew we didn't have a chance at Matt Christensen. I also learned right then that nobody wins in a 15-round battle with Coach K. Matt ended up signing at Duke for the 1995-96 season.

I could tell that recruits were sensing that something was wrong at BYU. I felt like our program was giving out bad vibes. There was growing discord within our coaching staff, and we were becoming less and less like a family.

One time Roger and I were out recruiting, watching a game. We ran into our old friend Jim Harrick, who was head coach at UCLA at the time. While were all checking out a 6-foot-7 guy, Coach Harrick turned to me.

"Hey Tony, ya looking for a job?" he asked.

"Well, if the right one comes along, I'd be interested," I replied.

"I've got a job I want you to keep your eye on," Jim said. "The University of South Alabama. I have it on good authority that there's going to be a change there soon. Keep your eye on that job, Tony." "Jim, I appreciate that tidbit," I said.

An hour later, Roger and I were in the car.

"What'd Jim say?" he asked me with an intense look on his face. "What'd Jim say?"

"Well, Rog, we were sitting there for two hours," I said, taken aback a little. "I don't know what you want."

"*You know damn well what I want*," he screamed suddenly. "*You know what I want!!* He was talking to you about another job, wasn't he? *Wasn't he?!*"

"You just worry about doing your job here," Roger continued. "Don't worry about getting any other job. I don't know why people have to go and backstab like that. Jim Harrick had better leave my assistant coaches alone!"

I was shell-shocked.

This wasn't the Roger I'd known for so many years. It was as if he'd gone crazy or something. I don't know what happened to him.

And the odd behavior continued. It hurt me because I loved Roger and his family so much. I hated to see him lose his mind like that.

As time went by, the situation at BYU became more and more uncomfortable. I became more and more measured and guarded around Coach Reid. I kept my mouth shut as much as I could. I just tried the best I could to be the best assistant coach in the world.

At the same time, I went into career preservation mode. I actively started looking around for other jobs. I wasn't that I was being disloyal; I wanted to put myself in a position to make a move if things got really bad.

Besides, I still had a dream of winning a national championship, and I was going to do whatever it took to reach that goal. No situation or circumstance was going to get in my way. No other person was going to be an obstacle in my path, and Roger Reid was no exception. The only person who could stop me was me.

During the summers, I reached out to other schools that advertised coaching vacancies. Once, I applied for an open head coaching position at the University of South Carolina. The assistant athletic director called my office number, and asked for Roger. Because our numbers were one digit apart, I knew he had misdialed while checking my references, and had reached me instead.

I drew a deep breath and went down the hall to Coach Reid's office.

"Rog, there's someone on the line from South Carolina," I said quietly. "There's a job open down there and they want to ask you about me." "About *you*?" Roger asked, incredulously. "You're no head coach. Why would anybody want to hire *you*? You can't even do your job around

here. That's a big time job, and they're interested in *you*?"

"Well, they want to talk to you about me."

I knew I had to stand there in front of Roger so that he wouldn't rip me behind my back. He gave very short, sharp answers: yes, no, yes, thank you, goodbye. And then he hung up the phone, wheeled around, and looked me in the eye.

"I can't believe what just happened to me," he said.

And I'll never forget what Roger said next. "Listen to me, big fella. I'll win with or without you. Don't you *ever* forget that."

Roger stormed out of the office, and drove off in his car.

I didn't get a call back from South Carolina. I kept hearing media reports and grapevine chatter that I made the top two, and that a lot of applicants dropped out of the running. Once I heard that, I followed up with the assistant athletic director.

"Tony, I know why you're calling," he said. "And I value our friendship, I really do. But I'll tell you what happened."

"Last Wednesday, we hired a new school president," he continued. "As soon as his press conference was over, he brought the athletic director, me, and the entire hiring committee into his office. 'We're not hiring no assistant coach,' he said. 'We're South Carolina, we're going to get us a name coach.'"

They ended up hiring Steve Newton, the head coach from Murray State. But the damage was done at BYU, and Roger intensely hated me from that day on.

In 1996, coming off another NCAA bid, we went 15-13. Our defense fell apart that year, and we didn't make the postseason. Alarm bells were going off all over the place. Color commentators on TV were chewing Roger out about the strange in-game decisions he was making.

And the fans and media knew that we didn't have a good team coming back for 1996-97, because we were getting beat out for just about every player we wanted.

There was an infamous incident when Chris Burgess, a highly-ranked recruit who happened to be a Mormon, picked Coach K and Duke over BYU. It was reported in the media at the time that Roger had told Chris that his decision had "let down all nine million members of the LDS Church."

For me, personally, there was a final straw. It came out of the blue.

"Tony, I've been thinking," he said one day. "I just might have to get myself some new assistant coaches."

Those words cut deeper than any knife or sword.

Even though he hurt me so badly, I still loved Roger. I still do. But I simply couldn't stand to be around him anymore. Roger didn't bring out the best in me, and he didn't help me reach my full potential to become the best coach I could be.

The only hope I had left was to reach the front door before the floorboards collapsed.

— — — — — —

The 1996-97 season started off disastrously. We lost our season opener at home to Cal State Fullerton by eight points. When we traveled to Washington four days later, the Huskies thrashed us 95-44. Our team's confidence was sinking lower and lower, and we were beaten by 22 at our place by the University of the Pacific.

We expected to be beaten by a Pac-10 team like Washington, but by teams from the Big West? The league that CSF and Pacific were in was considered a vastly inferior conference to ours. The only reason we scheduled them was to pump up our win total. But they sure did let the air out of us.

The only win we had that first month of the season was against Utah State at home, when we beat the Aggies 64-61. The lowest point came when we lost to Houston in the consolation game of the Cougar Classic (our own home tournament) by 20 points. Only 3,000 fans bothered to show up for that, and most of them were far gone by the end. BYU had a 1-6 record, and we hadn't even started conference play yet.

We had a week off after the Houston game, and I was happy for the chance to get away on a recruiting trip to Louisiana.

While down in the Bayou, I received a phone call at my hotel. It was Rondo Fehlberg, the athletic director at BYU.

"Tony, we have a mess on our hands," he said. "Compounding the problem is that we are really pressed for time. I'm not at liberty to discuss this in depth with you, but I'm calling to inform you that we have just dismissed Roger as head coach. We need somebody to coach the team for the remainder of the year."

"The media is swarming us from all sides," Rondo continued. "We need to do something *now*. As an administrator, I would like to offer you the interim head coaching position, with the stipulation that you will receive serious consideration for the head coaching position at the end of the season."

I couldn't believe what I was hearing. My mind was reeling.

My first thoughts were about Roger and his family. I was deeply worried about how they were taking this news. I knew that the head men's basketball coaching position at BYU was his dream job, and that he chased his dream as diligently as I was chasing mine. He was one of the winningest coaches in BYU history, and to be terminated this way was an embarrassing disgrace.

I also felt guilty. Most of the blame goes to the head coach when a team performs badly, but it's never exclusively his fault. Questions raced through my mind. What had I done to help bring this situation about? Could I have done better? Shouldn't I share some of the blame here? What will the players think? How will the boosters take the news of Roger's firing? How will the fans react?

"Coach Ingle, we are just a few minutes away from the press conference," Rondo said. "What will it be?"

"Nobody is going to win with this team," I replied straightforwardly. "If I say yes, then I'd be committing professional suicide. You're asking me to take the helm of the Titanic here."

"Coach, I know this is an extremely difficult situation," the A.D. said. "I know what kind of miracles it will take to get through the season. But we strongly believe that if anybody can hold things together, it's you. We really need your expertise and your experience as we go through this tough time."

I thought about our team. Players like Jeff Campbell and Matt Montague and Eric Nielsen weren't going to the NBA, but they were good players with good hearts. I'd recruited them. I knew I couldn't walk away from them now, I couldn't hang them out to dry.

It was becoming obvious to me what the correct course of action was.

"Tony, time's up," Rondo told me. "What's your decision?"

"I'll do it," I replied. "But only on one condition."

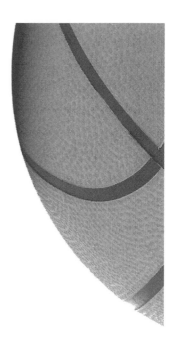

6
0-19

WHEN I TOLD BYU ATHLETIC DIRECTOR RONDO Fehlberg that I'd accept the interim head coaching position only if my win-loss record didn't determine my chances at earning the full-time job, I trusted him.

I had every reason to trust him. I figured that the administration knew full well the professional risk I had taken on. I assumed that my loyalty would be rewarded with fairness.

After I hung up the phone, I called Jeanne and gave her the news. She was happy and proud, but she knew what a difficult situation this was. She understood that my life was about to become much more busy and complicated.

"Jeanne, I don't know when I'm going to see you again, if it'll be this month or next," I said.

"That's okay," she replied. "Just remember to call sometimes."

I tried to call Roger to offer to help in any way I could, but he wouldn't pick up the phone.

I caught a flight from New Orleans to meet the team in Atlanta. We were scheduled to play another preseason tournament there, called the

Delta Airlines Classic. The other participating teams were Kentucky, Georgia and Georgia Tech.

When I arrived at the Marriott Marquis, the receptionist handed me an envelope full of messages. There were notes from every media source in the country, along with well-wishes from nearly every coach and scout I'd ever met.

The team arrived the next day, and I addressed the players for the first time as head coach.

"This is a difficult time," I said. "But we're a team, and we're going to stick together. We're going to fight to the finish, and we're going to conduct ourselves with class and dignity and always hold our heads high, no matter what the score is. And we're going to have fun."

That night, Delta Airlines organized a huge banquet for the players, coaches and fans of the participating teams. The room was filled to capacity, and each coach came to the podium to say a few words. My old friend Bobby Cremins from Georgia Tech went first, and he made a few comments.

Then it was my turn. As I tend to do in public speaking situations, I told a joke.

"There were two census workers traveling through the mountains of Kentucky," I began. "While wandering through the woods, they came upon an old country shack. When they knocked on the door, a little girl answered. One census worker asked her, 'How many people live in this home, little girl?'

"'Only me, Maw and Paw,' she replied. 'And my brother Bubba.' The other census worker asked if they could please speak to her parents. 'Maw and Paw ain't here, they're at the still back in the woods.' 'Well, where's Bubba?' the census takers asked. 'Bubba is at Harvard University,' she said proudly. The census workers looked at each other in disbelief. One said, 'You mean to say that you have a brother studying at Harvard University?'

"'No, sir,' she replied. 'They're studying *him*.'"

The crowd loved the joke, especially those Georgia and Georgia Tech fans in attendance. It was one of my old standards, so I raced through the joke not realizing that I had made something of a political mistake.

UK coach Rick Pitino came up to the microphone and pointed out that there were a lot of smart people in the Commonwealth of Kentucky. He took it well, though, and it was all in good fun.

It's probably a good thing we didn't have to play Rick's team in the tournament, though.

My first game as a Division I coach was against the University of Georgia, in the Georgia Dome, in my home state. My father and my sisters were in the stands, and they had driven down from Dalton to see me coach. I was so proud that they supported me like that.

The Bulldogs were nationally ranked, and we were giving them all they could handle. That was until Jeff Campbell, the only senior we had on the team, was hit in the eye with an elbow. It was a wound that would require six stitches.

We lost by 19 points, and I had no idea at the time what an ironic number that would turn out to be.

Our team couldn't afford any more lost time, and we'd already lost key players since the start of the season. Bryon Ruffner, our second-leading scorer from the previous season at 18 points per game, left school for personal reasons. Jarkko Ahlbom, our 6-10 center, sustained a season-ending knee injury in the second game of the year.

In addition to Jeff as the lone senior, we only had two juniors on the squad: Grant Berges and Justin Weidauer. BYU was suiting up eight freshmen, and we brought in three football players to fill out the roster. They had just helped BYU beat Kansas State in the Cotton Bowl. I called it the Tony Ingle Offseason Football Conditioning Program.

When we returned home to the Marriott Center for our WAC opener, we played San Diego State very tough. We had the lead with a few seconds left in the ballgame, but a defensive lapse allowed the Aztecs to tie things up and force overtime. We ended up losing 89-86.

We bounced back a week later to throw a scare into Rick Majerus' visiting Utah squad. That team was packed with future NBA players: Keith Van Horn, Michael Doleac, Andre Miller and Hanno Mottola. The Utes would make it all the way to the Elite Eight that season.

I remember that John Moala, a 6-9 Polynesian tight end from the BYU football team, was banging bodies with Doleac all night, giving him fits. Utah won by only 10 points, even though Van Horn scorched us for 37.

I really believe we would have come closer if we had a go-to guy who we could rely on for a key shot late in a ballgame. We just didn't have anybody who was a natural shooter.

Jeff Campbell had to leave that Utah game because of a back spasm early in the second half – he had such a hard time staying healthy that year. Michael Vranes, who'd go on to score 11 points per game the following season, had to end his season a week earlier because he required surgery to repair his right foot.

The Utah loss dropped us to 1-11 overall, and I hadn't coached our team to a win yet.

During the press conferences, I took all the blame for the defeats that were piling up. All I wanted to do was put a product out on the floor that our fans, boosters, alumni and administrators could be proud of. But I was becoming discouraged and demoralized, and I thought about quitting every day. I didn't want to let it enter my mind, but it did.

I am forever indebted to my assistant Russ Zaugg, who stuck by me the whole time. Greg Kite, a BYU legend who played many years in the NBA, came back to Provo in January to help me out as a second assistant because he loved the program so much. We all strived to control what we could, and we tried our best every day to improve our team.

And my players inspired me not to quit, because they didn't. They were being ridiculed in the newspapers, lampooned by cartoons. They were the targets of comments on talk radio and were abandoned by some of the fans, alumni, friends and boosters.

But those players stuck together, and never pointed fingers at each other – or at the coaches. Not a single player quit the team in mid-season.

In late January, I was asked to speak to a group of boosters at the Cougar Club. I stood in front of 300 people and delivered a speech about our team.

"These kids are working hard," I told them. "They have all kinds of adversity in front of them. But because they have pride in themselves, their families and their university, they're out there every day busting their butts. Anybody can cheer for a team when things are going good, but these guys are working hard and they deserve your support. They want to win... oh, they want so bad to win for you. But they're not failures."

"There's not a person in this room who hasn't failed at something at some point in their life," I continued. "Everybody here has experienced losses. So how can anybody look at my staff and my players and tell them that we're losers? We're not losers. Losers are people who quit. This team *will not quit.*

"The Mormon pioneers travelled over the plains and went through death, sickness and disease. They didn't quit. This team will not go through anything close to what they went through. But they're *my* Winter Warriors. They will fight until the end, I guarantee it. I can't guarantee you that we'll win a game this season, but these players will carry themselves with dignity and class whether they do or not.

"I've never begged anybody to come to a game, nor will I now," I concluded. "But they do deserve your support."

The Cougar Club gave me a standing ovation.

I got a letter from a booster a couple of days later. "I've been a member of the Cougar Club for 25 years," it read. "We've won a lot of championships and we've had a lot of success here at BYU. But you are the only head men's basketball coach to ever receive a standing ovation from our organization."

— — — — — —

I called Frank Layden, the president of the Utah Jazz, and asked him if he could speak to my team.

He told us about how when he was born, his mother died in childbirth. "I never had a mother for a minute," Frank said.

He had a tough childhood and faced a lot of adversity in his life, but Frank carries a card around that says, "You can't quit. It's a league rule." That's a quote from Brian Piccolo, the football player immortalized in *Brian's Song.*

Dale Murphy, the legendary Atlanta Braves baseball player and two-time National League MVP, also came in to give us a pep talk. He told our team to stay focused and always keep our eye on the ball. He lectured us on how to win with class but also lose with class.

LaVell Edwards, the BYU football coach, gave us the same kind of inspirational speech he gives his players at halftime. He talked about effort, togetherness and a never-say-die attitude.

Stan Watts, the Hall of Fame basketball coach who never had a losing season while at Brigham Young, talked to our players about how important it was to wear the BYU uniform. It was an honor, he said, to play for a team with such a great history. He told us that even though we were going through tough times, we needed to always be proud that we were part of a great tradition. He said that we were an important part of BYU history, because we were resilient and never quit.

Famed motivator Dr. Stephen R. Covey, who wrote the best-selling book *The Seven Habits of Highly Effective People,* gave us a lot of words of wisdom. He talked to us about principles and character and values. He told us to always be proactive, believe in a better future, and to never give up regardless of the odds.

It meant a lot to me that all these great speakers took the time to talk to our team. Each one gave us a great boost and fired us up. It made them players feel that what they were doing was important and meaningful.

On the court, we just tried to stay close as we could as long as we could.

We had a chance to beat Rice, but we threw the ball away late and lost by three points. That was January 23, and we wouldn't lose by single digits again for quite a while.

The Western Athletic Conference season felt as if it would go on forever. The league was as tough as it had ever been; four teams represented the WAC in the 1997 NCAA Tournament (with Utah, New Mexico and TCU earning No. 3, 4 and 5 seeds, respectively), and four more went to the NIT. Those were the glory days of the conference, when WAC teams were making the Elite Eight and pumping out NBA draft picks left and right.

While I was interim head coach, a total of 14 of the 19 teams we played were nationally ranked. I often wondered if our WAC championship teams would have been able to compete against a schedule like that. With my collection of banged-up upperclassmen, fresh-faced freshmen, and football players (some of whom had to be occasionally reminded about the rules of roundball), I felt like Richard Petty driving the Daytona 500.

In a go-kart.

Every night was an exercise in sheer survival. On February 3rd, we lost at New Mexico 74-32, and it was on national television. Billy Tubbs'

TCU team beat us by 40 at their place. When we went to Utah for a rematch, they drilled us 85-49. We were 1-18 overall, 0-10 in the WAC, and I was 0-12 as BYU's interim head coach.

We took our moral victories where we could find them. At 1-22 overall and riding an 18-game losing streak, we gave nationally ranked Tulsa a tough battle at their home arena. The Golden Hurricane had beaten UCLA, Oklahoma and Oklahoma State, and had won all 11 home games to that point. We had them tied at halftime, 32-32.

But then Eric Nielsen twisted his knee. Injuries just never stopped.

By February, there was only one storyline about our team, as far as the media was concerned. *"Are they going to win a game?"*

We had five of our last seven games at home, and everybody was trying to guess when the first victory would come.

It was an absolute circus. As the season drew to a close, reporters were calling day and night, trying to find out what was going on at BYU. Newspapers in Detroit and Denver and Boston wanted to talk to me, asking me if I had anything to say about whether or not I'd be the team's coach in 1997-98. Andy Katz was wearing me out.

And there were always the rumors about who was going to replace me when the season ended. When we played San Diego State for a second time, Aztecs head coach Fred Trenkle was asked repeatedly by the media what he thought about a potential opening at BYU.

"I'm the coach at SDSU now," he said coyly. "But at the end of the year, those decisions will be made."

I couldn't have hidden from all the innuendo and speculation if I'd wanted to. I had a TV show and a radio show to do each week, and fans and boosters called in with questions about me and the future of the program. There were interviews before the games, after the games too. Everywhere I went, someone was sticking a microphone in my face. It was difficult for our coaching staff to keep scouting and recruiting through all these distractions, but somehow we did it.

On March 1st, we had our final home game of the season, against Texas-El Paso. We were already eliminated from the playoffs, so we knew that this was our final shot at a win. Our record stood at one total victory against 25 losses, and I had presided over 18 of those.

Most teams in that situation might just pack it in and call it quits. But my Cougars fought for every minute of the game. They tried so hard

I DON'T MIND HITTING BOTTOM, I JUST HATE DRAGGING

to close the year with dignity. They wanted so badly to give me and the BYU fans at least one victory. It was the 25th anniversary of the Marriott Center.

We ended up losing to UTEP by five points that day. It was an improvement over the previous time; the Miners beat us by 34 at their place earlier in the season.

The season was over. As Doug Robinson of the *Deseret News* put it at the time, "The soap opera that included a firing, freshmen, futility, football players and freak injuries had drawn to a close."

But there were no tantrums, locker room outbursts, sulking, finger-pointing or belligerence. I was very proud of that.

The team went into the record books as the worst team in the history of BYU. But I can honestly say that no other team I've ever coached has ever worked as hard as that 1996-97 Brigham Young Cougars squad.

In our final team meeting, I told my players that they would be remembered alongside Danny Ainge's Elite Eight team among the great BYU storybook squads. This team was an object lesson that would be used in basketball camps everywhere, as an example of how to play with dignity, class, courage, hope, faith, and togetherness despite insurmountable odds.

We didn't win a single game, but I believe we won a lot of hearts.

— — — — — —

A local newspaper conducted a survey. They asked fans who they wanted the next head coach at BYU to be. A total of 34 percent wanted Danny Ainge. Another 34 percent wanted Tony Ingle. When the boosters were polled, I beat Danny by 15 points in a landslide.

On March 10, 1997, I had an appointment to meet with Dr. Merrill Bateman to discuss my future at the university. I had all these ideas I wanted to talk to the BYU administration about.

It never entered my mind that they'd even think about letting me go. I'd even spent the previous 10 days since the season ended out on the road recruiting. I was just going about my business, preparing for the upcoming summer and trying to get everything together for the 1997-98 season.

Dr. Bateman and vice president R.J. Snow came to my office, and I immediately started detailing my goals for the future.

As we rode down the main elevator and walked around the lower bowl of the Marriott Center, I started painting the picture for my vision of BYU basketball in the new millennium. I was talking about my ideas for the student section, for the booster club, and...

"Let's go up to your office," Dr. Bateman interrupted.

"But I didn't get to show you..."

R.J. looked at me. "Tony, don't," he said. "You heard the president, let's go."

We went back up the elevator, back into the office building. We walked into my office. R.J. sat down, and offered me a seat. I sat down.

Dr. Bateman began. "We're having a press conference in the morning, and you're not our coach."

"You don't have to flower it up," I managed to crack. "You can get right to the point if you want." "I just did," he replied.

"Well, I know this is hard for you to do, so..." "Oh, it isn't hard on me." There was a long silence.

"Well, then I won't waste any more of your time," I said, and I stood up.

"Tony, sit down," R.J. ordered. "You're emotional."

I really wasn't. I was as calm and rational as I had been five minutes earlier.

"Tony, there are a lot of things we need to talk about," R.J. said.

The shock was quickly wearing off, and I was a tangle of pain, nerves and anger.

"Listen," I said. "This is what *I* want to talk about. The agreement was that you weren't supposed to judge me on my win-loss record."

"We didn't," the president explained. "We used you as a benchmark to hire another coach."

"You're not looking at the positives."

I began categorically pleading my case, counting off the accomplishments with my fingers. "None of my players quit or told anybody I couldn't coach. Show me one article where the media said I wasn't a good coach. The booster club gave me their first standing ovation."

"And look at the attendance," I said. "Roger's last home game drew 3,000 people. In our last game against UTEP, we brought in 13,000. We had *13,000* people come to see a team that hadn't won a *single game* all year. The players are happy, attendance improved, the media's supportive of me, and the boosters are on my side."

"You have no other argument left, Mr. President," I said in conclusion, pointing my finger at him. "You judged me on win-loss record. That was the only thing I asked this school not to do."

"Tony," Dr. Bateman sighed, drawing a deep breath. "We did the best thing."

"You don't want me," I shot back. "And I know why. My daddy's a beer drinker. My daddy's a sot. I grew up differently than anybody who's ever been a head coach at BYU. I'm not good enough for you guys. I know it, and you do too."

"This all had to be done," Dr. Bateman said. "We did what's best."
"You did what's best for you," I said, and stood up to leave.

As I walked out of the office, I turned around. They flinched, as if I were going to physically attack them. I didn't, of course.

"Gentlemen," I said calmly. "If you ever want to win it all, give me a call."

———————

Driving back to our house in Orem, I was in a deep trance. All I could do was run that meeting on an endless loop in my head.

I tried to figure out why I chose such an audacious closing line. I wanted to let them know that I held up my end of the bargain. I believed that I had done the best job I could under the circumstances.

Besides, I still had that national championship I was chasing. Unfortunately for Dr. Bateman and R.J. Snow, it wouldn't happen at Brigham Young University. It was their loss, I thought to myself, and they had made a terrible mistake.

But I sat in our driveway for a long time in total silence, feeling like a loser and an utter failure.

I tried to figure out how I was going to tell my wife the bad news. She had been incredibly loyal for 23 years, and it didn't seem fair to put her and the kids through so much upheaval. In striving to protect individuals and institutions, I was hurting my own family, and the guilt was crushing my soul.

A million unanswerable questions washed over me. What were we going to do? Where would we go? What was I going to do for a living? Who in the world would ever hire a coach who went 0-19?

Finally, I worked up the strength and courage to walk through the front door. There stood my wife and children, who had been expecting daddy to come home with something to celebrate about. In anticipation of good news, Jeanne had even baked my favorite home-cooked meal of veggies and meat, and topped it off with some banana pudding.

I didn't eat a bite that night. I was trying so hard to hold back the cries and the tears that were ready to burst out of me. I wanted so badly to hug each one of them, but my entire body was numb.

All I could manage was a soft apology. "I'm sorry." Then I walked up to the stairs to our master bedroom.

I called my faithful assistant coach Russ Zaugg and told him what had happened. I thanked him dearly for his loyalty and selflessness, and I assured him that I would be a friend to him and his family whenever they needed one.

Then it occurred to me that I had to go back. If the press conference was in the morning, I needed to get out of the way of the new coach and pack up my things. When Jeanne came upstairs to check on me, I was putting my shoes and coat back on. I explained to her that I was headed back to the Marriott Center one last time.

When I went back downstairs, my family wasn't there. They were all out in the car waiting. "Daddy, let us come with you," the children said. "We want to help."

The ride to the Marriott Center was quiet and somber except for soft sniffling and sobbing.

We wasted no time in getting to work packing away all the evidence of my eight years at Brigham Young University. My kids pulled books off the shelves and took pictures off the walls, placed them in boxes and hauled them back to the car. It was a scene that broke my heart.

The press conference was the next morning, and Jeanne and I decided that it was best that we leave town for a while. So we took the children out of school and drove to Cedar City, Utah. We checked into a hotel and spent two days as a family there.

I DON'T MIND HITTING BOTTOM, I JUST HATE DRAGGING

The kids spent most of the time swimming in the pool and watching TV. They knew that mom and dad were hurting. And even though we made valiant attempts to hide the tears, it became overwhelming sometimes.

I truly believed that if I always strove to be honest, loyal, hard-working, positive, loving and God-fearing, if I knew my trade and performed my job well, then everything would come out alright for me. At the very least, I'd always have work and be able to provide for my family.

Wrong, wrong, wrong, on all accounts. Nothing could be farther from the truth.

And I was about to find out how wrong I really was.

— — — — — —

Whether or not their teams actually make it there, all college coaches go to the Final Four. The host city is also home to the National Association of Basketball Coaches' annual national convention. There are private coaching clinics, meetings, workshops and luncheons. There's also a whole lot of networking and handshakes.

My favorite part of the convention is always the NABC Guardians of the Game honors banquet. That's when all the annual awards are handed out.

In 1998, the Final Four was held in San Antonio. As I arrived there I contemplated the irony of the location. The Battle of the Alamo was a fierce struggle – the Texians knew they could not win against a superior force, but they bravely fought as hard as they could anyway.

It was the story of my life.

I took my son Golden to the convention, so he could see the greats of college basketball up close. He was like a kid at Christmas, watching all those players do the "heroes' walk" up to the podium to receive their All-American awards, their plaques and trophies. He loved every minute of it, and hung on every word of every acceptance speech.

Then it came time for the National Coach of the Year awards for each division of college basketball. As the ceremony continued, I sunk deeper and deeper into depression. I still hadn't been hired after a year. I watched all those great coaches walk up to the stage and accept their awards, make their speeches and pose for photographs.

And there I was, the worst coach in America, branded with an 0-19 record in his only opportunity at the Division I level.

I wondered how my son must have felt, sitting there next to the losingest coach in BYU history. I felt like a loser in life as well.

But Golden leaned over to me and whispered in my ear.

"I love you, daddy," he said. "One day you're going to be up there too."

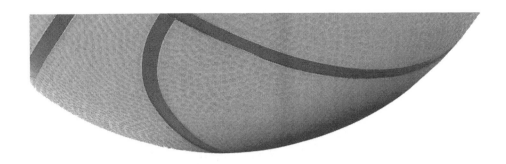

7
THREE YEARS OUT

AS I GO ABOUT MY DAYS, FRIENDS AND STRANGERS AND waitresses always smile and ask me how I'm doing. If you've been out of the house today, it's probably happened to you at least once or twice. Asking after others is one of those things that helps keep our society kind and civil.

When people inquire as to how I'm doing, I occasionally reply, "Un-be*lieve*able."

That's a good one; I suggest you try it. Watch how folks respond. You'll be able to read them like a book.

Some will wrinkle up their face and say, "Really? That bad?" Others will smile and go, "That good?" Saying one word, "unbe*lieve*able," is like holding a mirror to their face.

I try to mix it up. Occasionally I'll say, "I don't mind hitting bottom, I just hate dragging." That always gets a sympathetic laugh, except when it's a somber situation like a funeral or a hospital emergency room. Then it's just not appropriate.

Or they might say, "How ya doin', Coach?"

And I'll respond, "Today's the best day of my life."

When I was an assistant coach at BYU, before airline security was the way it is now, I flew into Minneapolis on a recruiting trip. I looked like an unmade bed. A worker at the airport asked me, "How are you doing this morning, sir?"

"Today's the best day of my life, thank you for asking." "Why? Are you getting a divorce?" he asked.

I got to the game and tried to find a seat in the bleachers. I asked somebody if a nearby seat was taken, and it wasn't.

"How are you today?" they asked kindly as I settled in.

"Today's the best day of my life."

"Really? Are you getting married?"

I couldn't believe it! I was divorced and married, all within the space of three hours.

It got me thinking about how everybody sees the world through their own eyes. Our outlook and attitude determine how we view the outside world, and we always have the opportunity to take a positive approach.

When I returned to Provo the next day, I walked into the Marriott Center. As I entered the elevator on the ground floor, a BYU fan passed me in the corridor on his way to the ticket booth. "Hey Coach, how're things going?"

As I pressed the button, I shouted, "Today's the best day of my life!"

As the elevator doors closed, I heard the man calling out after me, "You must have had a lot of bad ones!"

— — — — — —

After I was fired for going 0-19 as the interim head coach at BYU, Jeanne wanted to go on with our lives. But it seemed as though everywhere we turned, people were always bringing up how badly we were treated at BYU. People meant well, and they didn't mean any harm.

But our family just wanted to move on.

The town wouldn't let us, however. Months after BYU let me go, I found out that my son Israel was suspended from school. When I asked him why, he refused to tell me. So I tried again.

"Israel, why were you suspended?"

He just sat there at the table, looking into space, not saying anything. The third time I asked, more forcefully this time, he looked up at me with tears in his eyes.

"Dad, I'm not gonna tell you," he said.

I thought he was being disrespectful, so I pulled off my belt and gave him a couple of licks. I wanted to teach him to show more respect to his father.

A couple of weeks later, I learned why Israel was suspended. A young man at his school was making fun of me. "Your dad is a loser," the kid had told Israel. "Your dad couldn't even win a game. At least my dad has a job."

That sent Israel over the edge. And, I'm proud to say, Israel took care of business.

He was showing his daddy the ultimate respect by standing up for me. I have so much love and respect for Israel. I know that he loves me, and I also know that I didn't handle that situation properly.

Nobody was allowed to make fun of any of our family members - except for us, of course. I remember that Israel came up to me some time later and said, "Hey daddy, knock-knock!" "Who's there?" I answered dutifully.

"Owen," he replied.

"Owen?" I answered. "Owen who?"

"You're Owen 19."

At the basketball banquet following my 0-19 campaign, once the school had hired Steve Cleveland from Fresno City College as the new head men's basketball coach, BYU president Dr. Merrill Bateman stood up and thanked me for my service.

"Tony Ingle has a job at BYU any time he wants it," he told the gathering.

November 22, 1998 was a crisp Friday afternoon, the day before a big BYU football game against the University of Utah. I drove my car back to campus. I had been out of work for an entire year, my severance package had run out, and I needed money to feed my wife and kids. And Christmas was five weeks away.

It took a whole lot of swallowed pride to walk back there with my tail between my legs like that, but I didn't know where else to turn. I sat in my car in the parking lot for what felt like hours.

Finally, I walked into vice president R.J. Snow's office. "R.J., I will take that job," I said.

He replied, "What job, Tony?"

"The job Dr. Bateman talked about at the basketball banquet last year," I said. "He said that I had a job at BYU any time I wanted one. I'll take any job you have to give me. I'll do fundraising, I'll push papers at a desk, I'll sweep floors, anything you have for me. I've got to have insurance and benefits, and I need to provide for my family."

"I don't remember Dr. Bateman saying anything about a job, Tony. But I'll check on it."

I was shocked. I called R.J. back later that week, and I asked him about what the president had said. He told me President Bateman couldn't remember either.

Soon thereafter, I was having my semi-annual haircut at the BYU student center.

"So what are you doing now, Tony?" my friend Gary Dayton asked me as he settled me into the barber chair.

"I haven't found anything yet," I said.

"Tony, why don't you take one of those jobs Dr. Bateman said BYU would always have for you if you ever needed it?"

I wheeled the chair around. "You remember him saying that?"

"Dr. Bateman invited me to that banquet," Gary replied. "I cut *his* hair too."

Brigham Young University had completely shut the door behind me, and it hurt me deeply. But I tried to stay positive, and I put all my energies into finding another college head coaching job. I didn't want to be an assistant again, because I truly felt that my destiny was to coach a team to the national championship.

I knew it would be tough to find another coaching position. On my résumé, I put my combined eight-year record as an assistant and interim head coach (157-77). I listed our three NCAA Round of 32 appearances, and the fact that we won 21 or more games in six of the eight seasons I was there. I didn't include anything about 0-19, but it wasn't as if hiring committees didn't know.

Everybody knew the story about BYU's historic worst season ever, and that zero was seared into my forehead like a cattle brand.

But what surprised me during my job search was that 0-19 wasn't my primary obstacle. I applied at a public university in the Ohio Valley Conference that was part of a state system. There were six people on the hiring committee. During my interview, the president of the college walked in unexpectedly and took over the questioning.

"Coach Ingle, you went to Huntingdon College?" the president asked me.

"Yes, sir," I answered.

"That's a Methodist university, is that right?"

"Yes, sir, it is."

"Then you went to BYU, and that's a *Mormon* institution, if I understand correctly?"

"Yes, sir."

"So which side are you on?"

"Well, sir," I replied. "I have a lot of friends who are Methodist, and I have a lot of friends who are Mormon. In fact, I've got a lot of friends from a lot of religions. Let's just put it this way. On Friday night I'm with the Methodists. Sunday morning I'm with the Mormons. But when it comes time to party on Saturday night, I'm with the *Catholics*."

Everybody laughed, except for the university president. "I don't consider that very humorous at all," he said.

"I just don't want to make religion an issue," I explained.

But it was an issue. Very much so.

During the interview process for another position I applied for, they grilled me with more questions about the "Mormon Bible" than about basketball.

"I'd rather not talk about that in this particular context," I said. "I came here to talk about a job."

There was another head coaching position for which I didn't even get a callback. I dialed up the athletic director to ask them why.

"Confidentially, Tony," he said. "My president told me that there was no way we were going to hire no [expletive] Mormon."

———————

It was an extremely emotional event when Sunshine's boyfriend asked me if he could have my daughter's hand in marriage. I told him, "You can have her hand, and that's the only body part you're gonna get!"

I was still out of a job, and I had to come up with some money so that Sunshine could have the wedding of her dreams. As we all know, for every young woman a marriage ceremony is the Super Bowl, World Series and the Final Four all wrapped in one.

Finances were tight, so Jeanne and I took out a second mortgage and used the equity in our house to fund the wedding. There was no way that my daughter, my little cuppy cakey, was going to have a second-rate wedding day. No expense was spared in putting on a quality event that everybody would remember forever.

It was a happy moment for Sunshine, but it was a bittersweet and emotional time for her parents. Jeanne and I knew that our only daughter would no longer be in our home. She had flown the coop.

Meanwhile, my own mother was becoming quite ill. She smoked all throughout her days, and the tobacco took its toll on her body. In fact, my childhood physician Dr. Barnwell believed that the fatty tumor developed in my face because my mother smoked cigarettes all throughout the time she was pregnant with me.

Finally, mom contracted emphysema, and that's what ended up taking her life.

If I'd been coaching at the time, there would have been no way I'd be able to be there with her during her final two months on earth. For 70 straight days, while she lay in hospice care, my sisters and I sat by her bedside.

I wanted to guard her, the same way she protected me when I was a small boy recovering from multiple face operations.

When she died on January 27, her last words were, "I love my husband, I love my kids, I love everybody, and I love Jesus."

Those words meant a lot to me. Before she went off to be with Heavenly Father, the last name my mother spoke on this earth was that of

Jesus Christ. We never were very religious at all growing up, and the only time I saw her in church was when I invited her to come see Sunshine baptized in Dalton on Mother's Day. My mother had a deathbed confession, I guess that's what you could call it.

It was a very emotional time. I was always very close to my mother, and she had taught me to love myself and to always smile through the pain.

I jotted down a note in her memory. *"Life is short, serious and frail,"* I wrote. *"Learn from it, laugh at it, and live it well."*

— — — — — —

But for a while, I couldn't live up to my own lofty ideals. I was spiraling deeper and deeper into the D-word. I wouldn't allow myself to say the D-word, and I didn't let it enter into my mind.

Somebody once told me the story of a college professor who went off to study an African tribe, its language and customs. When he returned to his university in the United States, he noted that this tribe didn't have a word for "stutter" in their vocabulary. So nobody in this tribe stuttered. They didn't have the word for it, so they didn't know how to do it or what it was.

I took words out of my own vocabulary, one of which was "depression." I had frustration, I had discouragement. I was ticked off, peeved and pissed. I told myself that I was everything except depressed. If I didn't use the word for it, I wouldn't know how to do it.

I was mad at God. "Why did you let this happen?" I cried out as I prayed. "Why me? I didn't do anything wrong!"

I was prideful. My name meant a lot to me: Ingle. I worked hard to make sure that name was a good onr. Things never came easy, and I wasn't always perfect. But I felt like I deserved to get what I wanted, and what I wanted to do was coach basketball. I hadn't hurt anybody, and I hadn't done anything wrong that I needed to be punished for. I worked hard, and I lived right.

Each of us is only as good as our leaders, our talent, our resources and God will allow us to be. On those counts, I had done as well as possible under the circumstances.

I worked hard to put on a brave face, and I had a lot of jokes, quotes and anecdotes to give others the impression that I was okay. But deep inside, I was hurting and fighting depression. I lay in bed all day, holding little pity parties for myself. As the weeks dragged on, the primary highlight of my day was having a bowel movement.

Words can't express the devotion that my wife showed me during those times.

I was moping around all day, doing nothing. I remember that Jeanne said jokingly, "Are you trying to run me off or what? If you are, it's not going to work. You're stuck with me regardless."

Jeanne helped me stay focused. Because of her love, I knew I couldn't lay in bed and be miserable and selfish. But I was in a ditch, a deep trench.

And when you're in a rut like that, you have to be smarter and work harder to get up and out of it. I approached depression as if it was a real enemy, and I knew I had to fight like I was going to war. I had to change my thinking.

My main confidant during that time was my old friend Terry Lenahan. Friends like Chris Poulos, Dave Riley, Dave Hagan and Sam Swain helped me through those difficult times.

I remember getting an out-of-the-blue phone call from Dave Checketts, who was the president and CEO of Madison Square Garden. He gave me a pep talk, telling me to hang in there and never quit. The kind words of friends and associates gave me a better perspective about my life and my predicament, and each of them did their part to help me get up off the canvas and start punching again.

Through that process, I realized that "why me?" was the wrong question to ask. The "why" was very powerful, but I started asking "how." How could I improve? How could I get out of my own way?

I thought about all the things I'd accomplished in my life. I dug up the first trophy I'd ever won, from a basketball camp in 1968. Back when I won it, I put that trophy in a mayonnaise jar. When my sisters asked me why I'd done that, I told them the jar was my trophy case.

I found pictures of my time at Dalton Junior College and Huntingdon, and I wrote down my career accomplishments as a coach at Northwest, Southeast, Cherokee, Gordon College, Alabama-Huntsville and BYU. I found a pile of newspaper articles from big games we'd won, about cartwheel plays and battling for the Georgia 4-A championship and the Wendy's offense.

With all those notes and trophies and pictures and news clippings around me, I said to myself, "I guess I've had a pretty good life. Maybe I am worthwhile after all."

After that, I woke up every morning and I'd exercise by walking around the neighborhood. I'd come home, take a shower, and then I'd get dressed just as if I was going to work. For months, I put on a nice shirt and pressed pants, a tie and some shiny shoes, and I went down to my makeshift home office in the basement to try to plan and plot my life.

But I stared at the phone, trying to figure out who to call. It was like asking a girl out for the first time; the phone looked as big as a microwave oven.

I joined the National Speakers Association so I could fill my mind and heart with inspirational words, and so I could help people who were having hard times in their lives by sharing my own story.

It's a tough business to get started in, though. When you ask somebody, "Do you want to hear a great speech?" They might say, "Yes, sir." But if you follow up with, "So you want to pay me for it?" you usually get an altogether different response.

I remember flying to Atlanta with only two dollars in my pocket. Terry picked me up at the airport, lent me a car for the month, and let me stay at his condo for a month. I did some speaking engagements at major corporations and school systems. I did some conventions, conferences, after-dinner keynotes. I ended up being fairly successful at speaking. When I came back home to Provo, I had $2,900.

Steve Zimmerman at Champions Athletic Academy really came to my rescue. He gave me a consulting fee to help develop some ideas for CAA. We met a couple times a week, and he didn't put any stringent demands on my time. He gave me insurance and benefits, as well as an office and a phone.

But he was really giving me hope, inspiration and support.

I tried to help Steve and his academy the best I could. He helped me keep my self-respect and self-esteem up, and he also became a very good friend to my family during that time. There was no other way we could have made ends meet during those 18 months when I worked for CAA.

For a short time, I went to work for Fila as a golf ball salesman. After about six weeks of work, they called me into the office and tried to fire me. I told them that they couldn't, and I talked them back into hiring me for three more months. That took some salesmanship right there!

I did TV commercials for Debt Free Living. "Hi, I'm Tony Ingle," stuff like that. I still had a lot of name recognition in the state, and there was a study that 83.3 percent of Utahns knew either my name, my face or my circumstance. Astonishingly, only 64 percent could name both men who ran for President in the previous election.

My good friend Gregg Hayes hired me at Blue Ridge Carpet as a regional representative for the state of Utah. I sold commercial carpet, and I was able to get meetings because a lot of people in Utah knew me.

A lot of people don't know this, but two of the largest carpet buyers in the world are the Mormon Church and Marriott Hotels, which are both headquartered in the state, so it was a very lucrative gig. I felt bad because I wanted to do a good job for Gregg, but my heart just wasn't in it.

Any way I could make a dollar, I was willing to do it as long as it was righteous. I even did a comedy act at Johnny B's in Provo. "An Evening With Tony Ingle," they called it. Val Hale once said that I should get into comedy... and for one night, I did. I told all my old jokes, brought in some new ones, and the crowd loved them all.

I'm a fish when it comes to basketball. I live in it and I swim in it. I was able to stay close to the game during those times because Frank Layden let me scout some games for the Utah Jazz. I was grateful for the opportunity to be around the game I loved so much. It was also good for the résumé.

So was the other opportunity I took on.

Back when I was coaching at Cherokee High School, I helped promote the McDonald's All-American game. They had a little contest to see which coach could sell the most tickets. I took two days off from work and grossed $3,400 in ticket sales, and the next closest coach sold $129.

Then they asked me if I would serve as one of the hosts for the game, and that's where I was able to spend a day with the greatest college basketball coach of all time, 10-time national champion John Wooden of UCLA.

Coach Wooden and I kept in touch over the years. I called him from time to time, and he'd share his philosophies about basketball and life with me. I'd always take copious notes; I had legal pads full of them. I never made a big deal about my friendship with Coach, and for a long time the only person who knew I was calling him was Jeanne.

Years later, in the years after I was fired at BYU, I started the Utah Tip Off Club, modeled on the one in Atlanta. Our goal was to honor basketball players who had excelled both on the court and in the classroom.

Dale Murphy wrote the first donation check. For our first annual banquet, the Utah Tip Off Club board and I were looking for people to affiliate ourselves with. I had an idea, and went out back and called Coach Wooden.

"Coach, we're starting a basketball organization here in Utah," I said. "We're going to have a banquet at the end of the year. We'd like to give out two national Division I Coach of the Year awards, for men and women."

"I can't do it, Tony," he said. "I already have a Player of the Year award in my name, the John R. Wooden Award."

"No, Coach," I replied. "This would be for *coaches*. We'd like to present the awards under your name, and your wife's name as well. We'd like to call them the John & Nellie Wooden Awards."

He paused and said, "Tony, it would be the highest honor to have Nellie recognized like that. Because nobody's ever given her any credit."

We talked about it some more, and then he presented me with one stipulation.

"You can use our names, but as long as I'm alive, the women's Coach of the Year has to be a female," he said. I knew he was talking about the great women's coaches who happened to be male, like Connecticut's Geno Auriemma.

"After I pass, you can give it to anyone. But while I'm alive, it has to be a woman who receives that award. That's just the way Nellie would have wanted it."

We held a banquet every spring for five years. Craig Bolerjack from CBS was the emcee. Mark Eaton, the center for the Utah Jazz, was there one year, and Jazz team president Frank Layden came too. We flew Coach Wooden in on a private jet with his son Jim and his daughter Nan. We made sure that everything was first-class all the way.

Some of the coaches who won the John & Nellie Wooden Awards on the men's side were Clem Haskins, Rick Majerus, Mike Montgomery, Bill Self and Cliff Ellis. Jody Conradt, Pat Head Summit, Carolyn Peck and Kay Yow were some of our women's winners.

The awards were something I really loved being a part of. I was able to enjoy some quality time with Coach Wooden, and meet some of those incredible coaches from all around the country. It was too bad that after five years, after my family and I finally left Utah, there wasn't enough momentum or interest to keep it going.

— — — — — —

Even though I enjoyed small successes, there was an incredible pressure that kept dragging me down. I wanted to be happy for my wife and strong for my kids. My children knew I was hurting inside, even though I tried to hide it. My emotions and moods were affecting my entire family.

I remember driving down the street in our old Cutlass Ciera. I blurted out loud, "Life's bad."

My 14-year-old son Tony was riding with me. I'll never forget what he said.

"Life's not bad, daddy. It just gets a little tough sometimes."

Watching Tony and Israel and Golden play high school basketball really helped. Jeanne and I could always go to their games and watch them play, and it was a break from reality. Golden got a scholarship to play at Western Kentucky for Dennis Felton, and he was such a good shooter. A big reason why was that he spent so much time in the gym as a small boy, back during the Little Nuggets days.

But the ongoing situation kept Jeanne and I in a constant state of anger and frustration. We couldn't go to a restaurant without somebody coming up to us and bringing up the past. "Coach, I'm so sorry about what happened to you."

More to the point, we couldn't go to restaurants because we usually couldn't afford it. But one night, two and a half years after I had been released by BYU, we decided to splurge a little and go down to the China Bowl in Provo. Our spirits were in desperate need of raising.

We arrived at the restaurant at 9:45 p.m., because we knew the China Bowl closed at 10 o'clock and there wouldn't be too many people there.

We had a great Chinese meal. Afterwards, the waiter came with the fortune cookies.

Jeanne opened up her cookie, and the little slip read, "You are a most kind and honorable human being." There were all sorts of lucky numbers all over it too.

Then I cracked open my little fortune cookie, and there was no little white sheet inside.

I was so down and out, I didn't even have a future.

Jeanne and I looked at each other and started to laugh. It was the kind of powerful, deep chuckle that you can feel all over your body. I hadn't seen my wife laugh like that in years, and it did my heart so good to see her happy.

Looking back, I really think that was the turning point. Things started to get better after that.

I was asked by the SportsWest network to be a color commentator on basketball broadcasts for the Mountain West Conference, a new league that had split away from the WAC. My first practice came during a Snow College versus Dixie College exhibition junior college game, and I guess I did pretty well.

SportsWest signed me up for 10 games, and I was teamed with Tom Kirkland, and sometimes Dave McCann. They did the play-by-play while I snuck comments in from time to time.

One time, we did a game at the Thomas & Mack Center in Las Vegas calling a BYU-UNLV game. The game got close in the late stages. Nate Cooper jumped up and pulled down a key rebound for the Cougars. On the next trip down the floor, he got another rebound. And another one. "Gosh, I love Nate Cooper," I yelled out. "Nate Cooper is *tough*!" "Just how tough is he, Coach?" Dave chimed in.

"Nate Cooper is as tough as my mother-in-law's homemade biscuits!"

That quote really took off. Articles about that moment were written in newspapers all throughout the state, from Ogden to Salt Lake City to Provo. Everyone was talking about how well I was doing as a color commentator.

But for all the success and the compliments and the attention, it was hard being that close to the BYU team and not being able to get involved. I had a front-row seat, but I couldn't switch up the defense if I felt it needed to be changed. I couldn't substitute or call time outs or pull a player aside for a 20-second lesson. I missed coaching so badly.

Before my third game, which was between Air Force and UNLV, I called Jeanne.

"I can't do these BYU games anymore," I told her. "Some of these kids played for me and I recruited some of the others. I love them and know them. Seeing someone else coach this team is like watching another man dance with you. And you like it, you're happy another man's dancing with you!"

"Why don't you just do this game," Jeanne said calmly. "It doesn't have BYU in it. Then you can stop."

While we were setting up for the game at the arena, I let slip that it would be my last as a color commentator.

Dan Checketts of SportsWest was the brother of Dave Checketts, the CEO of Madison Square Garden. Dan came up to me when he heard the news.

"Tony, we've been meeting about re-upping your contract," he said.

"We love your work, and we'd like to give you $250 more per game."

"I need the money, but my heart's not in it," I said. "I'm sorry, Dan."

When I called Jeanne back that night, she asked me to change my mind.

"Tony, we need the money," she pleaded. "You know I wouldn't ask you to do it. If you don't want to do it, you know I'll support you. But we really need that cash."

I ended up staying, and called all 10 games for SportsWest. I could never say no to Jeanne.

Despite all the odd jobs that I had strung together, our household financial situation wasn't improving. The bills were mounting higher and higher, creditors were calling all the time, and the kids knew full well that things were really tough.

Because of the inconsistencies in our income, I had a credit card with $30,000 on it at 28 percent interest. The bank threatened to foreclose on our house. I was told that my best strategy was to declare bankruptcy. Our house was treated as a foreclosure case, but I never went bankrupt. No matter how bad our finances were, I knew I couldn't let the bank gain control of our lives.

I DON'T MIND HITTING BOTTOM, I JUST HATE DRAGGING

Jeanne wanted to go to work, but I still wouldn't let her. She begged me. Our children were in high school then, and she'd been there for them for their whole lives, and I knew she wanted to be there for them too. The teenage years are tough for anybody, and I wanted to make sure that the kids had at least one parent around to keep an eye on them, help them with homework, or act as a shoulder to cry on.

So we tried to make do with less of this and much less of that so that she could always be home with the kids.

We were down to one car, that 1985 Cutlass Ciera, which we shared among six drivers. We had so little money that we went for over four months without car insurance. It was very scary with four teenagers with new driver's licenses, out there on the road without any coverage, but we simply couldn't afford any insurance.

When Eliott or Golden ran out the door to drive somewhere, we'd call out after them, "Be very careful!" I don't know what we would have done if they'd have ever hit somebody, and I'm glad we never found out.

One day, it got to be too much. I finally surrendered. I went down to the basement of our home and I hit my knees.

"Heavenly Father, I'm all yours," I prayed. "I'll let go of my pride. Whatever you want me to do, I'll do it. If you want me to go back to high school or be a junior college coach, I'll do that. I'll even be an assistant. I give myself completely over to your will. Just let me know what you want me to do."

When I got up, I felt that burning inside me. It was that comfort that the missionaries had told me about when I learned how to pray all those years ago at Jeanne's house in Dalton.

I was so inspired that I got some 3x5 index cards and wrote down my thoughts, which I then taped above my office desk. The father of one of Israel's friends went to use my phone one day; to my surprise, he took the index cards and Xeroxed them. He went to Wilkinson's Trophy Company and had a plaque made for me. This is what the plaque said:

Today is beautiful, and I will make it the best day of my life.

Today is going to be a day I'm going to need to show faith.

Today will present something that will cause me to laugh and be happy. Today I will be a miracle of love in action, thoughts of purity, and visions of success.

Today is so precious and full of memories of loved ones that have passed.

Today is a day to learn and grow and improve my life for the better.

Today is a day to be a hero, and help others find good in themselves.

Today is a day of awareness, or just how frail life really is.

Today I will see more clearly into my true purpose of life.

Today is the right time to commune with God and His universe.

Today is a day to live a high quality of life for others to emulate.

Today, with help from family, friends and God, I can face anything.

— — — — — —

Bobby Cremins called me a few days later. "Tony," he said. "There's a job opened up down here in Georgia, an hour north of Atlanta. Kennesaw State. I know a lot of people up there. I can help you get it." "I can't apply for any coaching job right now," I replied.

"You've *got* to be kidding me, Tony," Bobby said. "You need to coach again. I can hear it in your voice, you're miserable."

"But Tony is going to be a senior next year, and Israel's going to be a junior," I explained. "I can't move 2,000 miles away. They'd have to make friends all over again, and they're quiet, reserved kids. I've already hurt them enough, Bobby. I'll get back into coaching once they're graduated."

"That's nonsense," Bobby said. "That all sounds like a pack of excuses to me."

When we hung up the phone, I went upstairs to the master bedroom.

My son Eliott passed me on the stairs.

"You going to apply for that job?" Eliott asked.

"I don't know what you're talking about," I replied.

"I overheard you and Bobby talking," he said. ""You need to practice what you preach. You've always said to chase your passion, not your pension. You're scared, daddy. That's why you don't want to apply."

Later that night in bed, Jeanne asked me who had called. I gave her a list of some of the people I had talked to over the course of the day. I neglected to mention one.

"I heard Bobby Cremins called about a coaching job," she said. There was no hiding anything from the Ingle family grapevine.

The next night, I was sitting in the kitchen watching *SportsCenter* on ESPN. I had a bowl of chili, Doritos, a tall glass of A&W root beer and my favorite Double Stuffed Oreo cookies all laid out on the counter. Those cookies were some of the key weapons I used to fight my depression.

Israel and Tony came into the room. "Hey dad, can we talk to you?"

Prom was coming up, and there had been some talk about preparations earlier in the day. I thought they wanted to talk about tuxedos and corsages or something. Maybe even limousine service. In any event, it had to be something that cost money, I was sure of it.

So I turned the TV volume down so I could still watch *SportsCenter* out of my side-eye.

"Daddy, turn it off," Tony said.

I grumbled, because they were just getting to the basketball highlights. I reached over and hit the button on the remote.

"We heard a job opened up in Georgia," Israel said. "Are you gonna apply for it?"

"No," I replied flatly.

"Why, daddy?" Tony asked.

I didn't want to tell them it was because I was thinking of their own interests. I didn't want to put them through a cross-country move at that crucial juncture of their lives.

But I really didn't want to tell them the *real* reason: that I felt like a failure and didn't want to go through the humiliation of being turned down. In just a few short words, Eliott had been correct in his assessment of the situation. I *was* scared.

But I didn't say any of that.

"Timing's not good, son," I managed to say. "The timing just isn't good at all."

"Well, daddy," Israel said. "Me and Tony have been talking about this. We know what you told Bobby on the phone... but we'd rather see you coach than us play."

I lost it. I just bowed my head and cried. I knew how much they loved basketball. When they told me that, I knew exactly how much they loved their daddy.

How lucky I was, to have children so selfless and devoted. The two of them came around the counter to embrace me. Tony put his arms around one side of me, and Israel put his arms around the other side.

But through the tears, I checked to see where their hands were. I didn't want either one of them stealing my Oreo cookies.

———————

I called Kennesaw State the next morning.

The athletic director at Kennesaw, Dr. Dave Waples, answered the phone. I was shocked that an A.D. would pick up at a published number, I'd never experienced that in all my years of coaching.

"I'm Tony Ingle, and I'm inquiring about the head men's basketball coaching position," I said. "Before I do, I want to make sure that it's open. I don't want to waste your time or mine."

"It's open," he replied. "But we're closing it next week."

I told him my story. I told him I'd last coached at BYU, and that I coached at a high school about 20 miles from Kennesaw. The head track coach at KSU was the assistant track coach at Cherokee all those years ago.

I told him about my 0-19 season, about my three years out, and I even told him the story of what had happened the previous night with Tony and Israel.

Dr. Waples said, "I can assure you, Coach Ingle, that as long as your résumé gets here on time, it will be given very serious consideration."

After I hung up the phone, I went downstairs to my home office and took out my money jar. I put the pennies, nickels and quarters in piles, and there was just under three dollars.

That was how broke we were.

Jeanne and I were overdrawn on our checking account. We had nothing in savings. So I brought my last $2.90 down to the post office.

I put that change on the counter, and sent my résumé to Kennesaw State in a Priority Mail envelope. I mailed it on a Thursday and it arrived in Georgia the following Monday.

When I visited campus for my interview, I couldn't believe how beautiful it was. I remembered Kennesaw State as a little junior college. It had grown into a big, gorgeous campus, with steel and glass buildings everywhere.

A week later, on April 26, Dr. Waples called me to tell me I had the job.

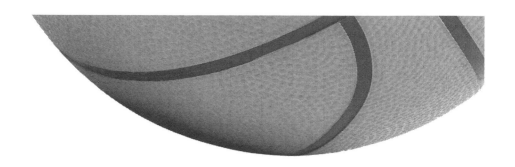

8
SECOND CHANCE

WHEN I ARRIVED ON KENNESAW STATE'S CAMPUS, I brought my four key attributes with me: my faith in God, my belief in myself, a spirit to serve, and courage to continue. I had been through so much, I knew I had the strength to endure to the end.

But the most important thing I brought with me was my dream. I was determined to win a Division II national championship. I knew there was a national championship in me, and not just one. It was a do-or-die thing for me, and settling for second place wasn't going to be good enough. Not that there's anything wrong with second place, mind you. Sometimes the second rat ends up with a little bit of cheese.

As I drove east, I brought that Kansas sunrise with me.

I felt like a caged tiger. I had been out of the business for three years, and I was going to prove that I was a good coach. There were plenty of people who had told me I wasn't good enough.

I had close friends and people in leadership positions that told me, "Hey Tony, don't you think you might not be cut out to be a college coach? Maybe you should go back to coaching high school kids." I brought all that with me.

There's an old saying in the South that you don't tell anybody your "go-up" goals, because they turn into "blow-up" goals that blow up in your face. I don't believe that. I told my "go-up" goals to everyone.

"I have high ambitions and high dreams for the Kennesaw State Owls," I said at my first press conference. "I want Kennesaw State to be the most talked-about basketball program in the state. I want people in the community to feel like it's their program. I pulled up on campus and saw University of Georgia G's on the front of people's cars. I'd like to see a day when people are proud to put a K on the front of their cars.

"No college in the state of Georgia has ever made it to the final four of the NCAA Division II tournament," I continued. "We're not going to sacrifice any principles. We're not going to hook and crook, or cheat and lie. We're going to build a solid foundation to support the castle of our dreams. In the end, we're going to be the first university in Georgia to win an NCAA national championship in basketball."

But the more I kept talking about national championships, the more people laughed at me and ridiculed me. Here was a guy who had just pulled into town in an old Cutlass Ciera with a big horn and no hubcaps. That car had so much rust, you needed a tetanus shot to ride in it. It was smoking, and by that I don't mean "smoking hot." People gave me money to drive around their neighborhood and kill the mosquitoes.

So when I started talking about winning it all, it was like they just patted me on the head and said, "That's nice, Coach."

It certainly wasn't that people didn't believe that Kennesaw State couldn't produce a national championship team. The baseball, softball and women's soccer teams were Division II powerhouses, and each had won national titles.

But I was a coach branded as a loser with an 0-19 season, taking over a men's basketball program in shambles, a team that had earned a place on the university's athletic totem pole at the bottom, behind golf and tennis.

My son Eliott and I drove cross-country together from Utah to Georgia, and we made it in less than three days. I left on a Friday, and started work on Monday morning.

Jeanne stayed in Orem because Sunshine was pregnant with her first child, our second grandchild. On June 17, six days after old Papa Tone's birthday, a beautiful baby boy named Jaiden entered into the world.

There were so many new beginnings in our lives that year. It was a new millennium, I had a new college coaching job, and I was a grand-daddy to boot.

But when I came back from my trip to Utah to meet Jaiden, our family still didn't have a Georgia address. I slept on my office couch from May 1 until August 9, when Jeanne came out to be with me. I didn't have a pillow, so I used some balled-up t-shirts. I took showers in the locker room, and washed my clothes in the laundry. I would work until 2 o'clock in the morning, take a little nap, then be back awake and ready to go at around 5 o'clock.

Stephen Covey always says, "Begin with the end in mind." When I began trying to build Kennesaw State into a national champion, I was starting from scratch. The coaches before me had taken all the books and records. So I was working day and night trying to put things together. I ordered equipment, organized summer tryouts (which you can do in Division II, not Division I), and interviewed the returning players. At first, I had no assistant coaches to help me recruit, schedule or help run summer basketball camps.

I got on that phone and started dialing. I had plenty of contacts in the area. I'd grown up close by, coached at Cherokee High School and Gordon College, worked at the Atlanta Tip Off Club, and people still remembered the Little Nuggets. When up and coming young coaches in the area heard I'd taken the job at Kennesaw, they called me up and asked me if I was hiring.

One of them was Stace Tedford, who applied in May. I noticed that Stace had Lenny Acuff listed on his résumé; Lenny was my assistant at Alabama-Huntsville and had since become the head coach there. Coach Acuff had a lot of nice things to say, so I called Stace in for an interview.

He was fresh-faced, right out of college. When I asked Stace if he was married, he told me he wasn't.

"I want to build a solid team here at Kennesaw," I said. "If you're married, then I know you understand what it is to be on the best kind of team that could ever be. There are a lot of players who come from single-parent households, or without daddies, that never got a chance to understand that, so I want my coaches to provide examples of leadership and commitment for them. So I can't hire you if you're not married."

"Well, I'm not married *yet*, but I'm getting married in June," Stace replied. "June the 28th is my wedding day."

"I'll give you serious consideration," I said. "You can come work our camps in June. When I see that ring on your finger, I'll hire you."

So I hired Stace Tedford at the very end of June. I can't say enough about Stace. He drove the bus, handled the finances, ran camps, organized the booster club, wrote thank you notes and did public relations work. I hate to rank any of my assistants over any other, but nobody I've ever had on my bench has worked harder or more diligently than Stace did during that time.

When Dr. Waples gave me my budget that summer, he also presented me with a choice. I could have one assistant coach and a secretary, or two assistants.

"This is your money, you decide," he told me.

"I'd rather have two coaches, sir, if you don't mind," I replied. "A secretary can't run passing drills."

I kept running into Jeff Jones, an assistant at a junior college in Florida, on the recruiting trail. He was an encyclopedia of knowledge on high school players in the South. I finally asked him if he would be interested in coming to work at a Division II college, and his eyes lit up. I met his wife and children, and I took him on.

I hired Jeff on August 10, and school started on the 15th. The season was fast approaching, and I just hoped we were ready for it.

Stace, Jeff and I put the Owls team together the best we could. But when the players came in to practice, they were so out of shape it was pitiful. When we ran drills, I could smell smoke on some of the players. In one drill, I asked our 6-7 inside player to stand on the low block.

"Coach," he responded with a quizzical expression. "What's a block?"

I shook my head in disbelief. I asked out loud, "These people call themselves basketball players?"

Before the season, I gathered my assistants together. "We're all going to wear coats and ties on the sidelines," I told them.

This was Division II, where assistants (and most head coaches) usually wear polo shirts with school logos on them, so they were incredulous.

Coats and ties?

"Let me tell you something," I said. "People go to church every Sunday wearing suits. There are only 52 Sundays in a year, so those are pretty special days, right? We've got 26 ballgames this season, and those are pretty special at my house."

Any injured players or redshirts on the Kennesaw State bench had to suit up too. A lot of those kids had never worn a tie in their lives, so I enrolled them in an etiquette class that the student government had organized. There were lessons on how to hold a fork, how to hold a spoon, and how to turn your cup over if you don't want coffee.

We knew we probably wouldn't win a lot of games that first year, but we were going to be the best-looking, most well-mannered team in the Peach Belt Conference.

— — — — — —

I tried to do some fundraising over the summer. I asked the lady in charge of marketing for the athletic department how many season tickets they had sold the previous season.

Four, she replied.

"Four *hundred*?" I responded. Our Spec Landrum Center seated 1,000, so 400 would have been a decent percentage of sold seats.

No, she told me, Kennesaw State had sold four season tickets the year before. Four as in *four*. When she let me see the books, I noticed that three of them had the same last name.

"If you don't mind, could you tell them not to sit together?" I asked. "It'll look like we have more people if they spread out."

When it came time for my first game as the head coach at Kennesaw State, my assistants and I came out on the floor in our coats and ties. My team had on brand-new black and gold uniforms. We were looking good, looking sharp!

But there were more people on the court during warmups than there were in the stands. I found out that nobody was even taking money at the door, so people could walk right in and watch the game for free if they wanted. And very few people did.

I went to the scorer's table before the game. "Hey Grant," I said to the P.A. announcer. "Why don't you introduce the crowd, we'll get started quicker."

Early on in that first season, a friend of mine called me and asked when that night's game started.

"How long will it take you to get here?" I replied.

I was going to find 1,000 people to come to our games if I had to tap dance at halftime, and I was determined to drum up support for KSU basketball in the local community. So I put together a list of all the millionaires I knew in the state of Georgia: businessmen, folks in the carpet business, anybody I knew who'd been successful. I called them asking for donations.

A lot of them did end up donating. Some of them were better friends with their money than they were with me, and didn't donate. But that was okay, because I raised enough to get the program started.

I kept bringing checks in to a happy Dr. Waples, and I told him my plan. "I want to start a booster club here at KSU," I said. "I want to call it the 100 Club, we're going to try to find 100 people to make major donations to help build the foundation of this program."

With the help of our new booster club, we started to create a small swell of support over the course of my first season at Kennesaw. Once our coaching staff had figured out who the serious ballplayers were, we played hard every night and hustled and scrapped. More and more fans showed up to see the Fighting Owls play.

We won 11 games during that 2000-01 season, but KSU missed out on the Peach Belt Conference playoffs.

Golden had been away from the family for a year, out at Western Kentucky playing for Dennis Felton after attracting Division 1 interest as a Nike All-American. He went to the NCAA Tournament with the Hilltoppers, and he loved playing there in Bowling Green.

But there was some friction, because he was considering going on a two-year LDS mission. WKU gave him no guarantees that there would be a spot for him on the team when he came back. So Golden started making overtures to me, floating the idea about coming to play for us.

It was a tough spot, though. Roger Reid had two of his sons play for him at BYU, and it wasn't the most positive experience. I never experienced it myself, but I've seen first hand how tough it is to be the coach's son on a team. The coach might not hold his son to a higher standard, but it's always a different standard; at the very least, the knowledge that one's own flesh and blood is out there on the floor is always at the back of a coach's mind. Sometimes the other players feel resentment, and sometimes they feel as though they're not being treated fairly. For a coach, having your own family on the roster can split a team in half, and it can turn into a volatile situation.

But we ended up with Golden. Honestly, I think he came to Kennesaw because he wanted to help his dad. He loved me and believed in me, and he knew we needed a point guard. And I was more than happy to have him around.

He was able to run the team for us. He could shoot and pass, and we had another small guard named Ed Womack who could really let it fly. Golden and Ed made a great tandem in the backcourt.

I had to recruit to my strengths, and that meant bringing in players from the Utah high school teams I'd spent so much of the previous years watching. We signed Hala Kaufusi, who played at Provo High School. Hala had played on some teams with Golden, so they already knew each other. We got a 6-8 power forward named Travis Visentin, as well as Brandon Moore, a guy who could flat shoot the lights out.

I'd been away from Atlanta for over a decade, so I didn't know the city well anymore. Besides, every time Coach Jones or Coach Tedford or I would show up to a game, they'd laugh at us. "Kennesaw State? You've got to be kidding me."

We scheduled meetings with players and their parents. Player after player would tell us, "I'm coming, I'm coming," and they were lying to us. They'd call and tell us they were on their way to the gym to meet with us, and we'd stand outside waiting for them.

They wouldn't even show up.

Hardly anyone had heard of Kennesaw, and those who had knew Kennesaw as a former NAIA school that only had three 20-win seasons in its 15 years of fielding a basketball team.

We tried anything to get the word out. My assistants worked the campus groups to stir up support so we could have a full gymnasium, and we had a "Midday Madness" celebration for our first October practice. We brought in the cheerleaders, served food, then we gave everybody schedules and asked them to come to games. We held it at lunchtime while everyone was on campus, instead of at night when everybody was asleep at home. If we had a "Midnight Madness," we would have had a strobe light and a big power bill, but only five or six people would have shown up to see it.

I started a TV show on local cable that was shown in four or five counties. I did the show from my locker room, and I tried to get people to call in and ask questions. I had a radio show too. I was wheeling and dealing, blowing and going. I was selling our basketball program 24/7.

We started off the season slow in that second year. I called my new part-time assistant, Greg Matta, into my office. I asked him what our record was.

"We're 2-5, Coach," he answered.

"Are you ready for this?" I responded. "I'm gonna teach you something. The inmates are about to run the prison."

Coach Matta was perplexed. "What do you mean by that?"

"This team is not willing to follow my lead," I said. "They don't have what it takes, man for man, to be champions. Now, before you look at me and think I'm negative, let me tell you what's gonna happen. Don't say a word to anyone else, just lay back and watch it unfold. We are probably going to win 20 games, get in the conference finals, and lose. We won't make it to the NCAA tournament, but we'll come close."

Kennesaw State finished the 2001-02 season with a 20-10 record. We lost in the Peach Belt league championship game to Augusta State (our fourth game in five days), and missed an automatic berth in the national postseason by 12 points.

I found out later that the night before the championship game, a couple of guys from the starting five stayed up all night drinking. They were celebrating that they made it to the finals, and that was good enough for them. They were simply happy to be there.

After the season, Coach Matta came up to me again. "You were right about how the season was going to play out, Coach," he said. "How did you know?"

I'd known something was brewing early in the season. I backed off and didn't discipline the players that much, knowing that particular group of guys couldn't take the pressure required to go all the way. There were a few on the team I knew could handle it, but the majority of the players weren't willing to follow our coaching staff through the hard grind required to forge champions.

So I just let them play. I knew that would get them to a certain plateau based on their combined talent, and that they'd had the ceiling eventually. And they did. It was only the fourth 20-win season in school history, and 2002 marked the first time that KSU had won Peach Belt tournament games (three of them) since going from NAIA to Division II, but I knew it was fool's gold.

We needed to find more players that would meet national championship criteria.

———————

That spring, our staff worked hard on the recruiting trail, harder than any staff I've ever had, before or since. Coach Jones brought in Reggie McKoy, who averaged a double-double in junior college and finished eighth in the nation in rebounding. During that time, Coach Tedford closed the deal on the greatest go-to guy in Kennesaw State history, a young man named Terrence Hill.

As a Division II school, we got lucky with Terrence. He was MVP of the Alabama junior college state tournament, and was a solid mid-major Division I prospect. Stace and Jeff got in on him early. When Terrence narrowed his list down to four, it included D-I schools Central Florida and South Alabama, as well as Ray Harper's Kentucky Wesleyan program, which had recently won two D-II national championships. Then there was us.

Central Florida dropped its offer when a highly-ranked high school guard committed. The next weekend, Terrence went to visit South Alabama. But during Terrence's campus visit, the school fired head coach Bob Weltlich, which effectively wiped out the program's recruiting list.

And while Terrence was on the South Alabama campus, guess where Tony Ingle was? I was in Fort Payne, Alabama, in his mother's front room eating barbeque chicken, watching the NBA playoffs. Terrence came back to the house, but he told me that he was leaning heavily towards Kentucky Wesleyan.

But two weeks later, we had Terrence Hill.

Like I said, Coach Tedford sealed the deal. He swooped in and worked overtime to sell that young man on what Kennesaw State could offer him.

Terrence's high school team was 31-3 in his senior year of high school. His sophomore year in junior college, his team was 31-4. In short, he knew about winning. I told him that I wanted KSU to be the first NCAAaffiliated team – Division I, II or III – to win 30 games. Life University had won 30 games in a season during its run of four NAIA championships, but an NCAA team hadn't done it yet.

We had a scorer and a rebounder, and then we added Tommy Thompson out of my hometown of Dalton. Tommy would not back down from any challenge, I'm convinced he would fight a buzz saw with his lips. I signed a 6-6 player named Georgy Joseph from Florida after seeing him on a game tape; I had been scouting somebody else on that tape, until I found out Georgy was originally a track star who could run the half-mile in a minute and 51 seconds.

"I used to have a 1960 Chevrolet that couldn't even do that," I remarked.

I knew we had something going. I knew that we had a chance to do something good that year.

A big part of the reason we had such a great recruiting class was that I had an ace up my sleeve that a lot of other colleges couldn't trump. How many universities in the South, especially Division II schools, get to take a trip to Hawaii?

I had gone to Dr. Waples that spring to lay the groundwork for the master plan. "Sir, I want to take my team to the Hawaiian Islands," I said. "I'm not asking you for the money, I just want permission."

"You're going to raise the money to go to *Hawaii*?" he asked. He thought I was out of my mind.

My plan was to raise $30,000, enough to fly 22 people out to Hawaii for one week, which would include three games. I was confident that I could get the 100 Club to donate the money, so I signed an agreement. I promised Dr. Waples that if I didn't raise the funds, then it would come out of my own pocket.

We raised the money, got a great deal on flights, and booked the trip. I can't say conclusively that the Hawaii trip was the reason why we were able to land great players like Terrence, Reggie, Tommy and Georgy. But I will say this: it sure didn't hurt.

— — — — — —

We were compiling ingredients for a great season, but something was suddenly missing. We didn't have a point guard.

Golden was struggling with a key life decision. He had been thinking about going on his two-year LDS mission for a while. He was planning to go after his freshman year in college at Western Kentucky, but he chose instead to come to Kennesaw to help me establish the program. But a strong and undeniable urge was building up in his heart to serve the Lord Jesus Christ.

So he asked me if he could leave the team. I obliged, because I knew full well that spiritual priorities outweigh the physical. I had a backup plan for my team, but late in the summer I found out that the point guard we'd signed didn't make his grades.

Coach Tedford and Coach Jones came to me in my office that August.

"We're looking everywhere for a point guard," Stace said. "You've got one sitting at your house, one who just so happened to average 16 points per game for us last season."

"I can't ask him to change his mind," I replied. "This is important. Golden has been planning for this his whole life."

"Could you at least ask him, though?" Jeff inquired.

I promised my assistants I would try. One night, I explained Kennesaw State's predicament to Golden. I told him about the point guard who had fallen short of KSU's academic requirements.

"I just want you to be aware of the situation," I said. "Please think about it."

I tried to word it as gently as I could, but there's no way to properly attach a pillow to a sledgehammer. That's a lot of pressure on a kid.

"Dad, I'll think about it," Golden said.

A day went by, and then another day went by, and yet another. I couldn't sleep because I knew how hard this was on everybody involved.

I was fighting to keep my own priorities straight. We have a tendency to put our family first, but it's always more important to put faith first. I tried to remind myself of that.

One day, I was up early, at 6 o'clock in the morning. Golden came walking into the kitchen.

"Dad..." he began.

"Good morning, Golden!" I exclaimed nervously.

I DON'T MIND HITTING BOTTOM, I JUST HATE DRAGGING

"Daddy, I just want you to know..."

His chin started to tighten, and tears formed in the corners of his eyes. I knew what he would say, but I let him finish.

"I've been praying all night," Golden said. "I couldn't sleep at all. You know I love you, daddy, but you've told me that you're my earthly father and that you're imperfect. But I have a Heavenly Father who *is* perfect. And I love my Heavenly Father. I'm going on a mission, daddy.

I'm sorry."

I gave him a big hug, and I was crying too. "You don't have to apologize," I said as I held my son in my arms.

"I know you needed me, or you wouldn't have asked me," Golden said through the sniffles and tears. "I love basketball, daddy, and I know how much basketball means to you. But I've prayed, and I know that this is what I need to do. I just *know* it."

"There's someone in the mission field that needs you more than I do," I replied. "The Owls will be alright, we'll find a way. I love you, Golden."

"I love you too, daddy."

———————

In the early part of the 2002-03 season, Kennesaw State went out to Hawaii and won two out of three games. We beat Chaminade, Hawaii Pacific, and we lost to BYU-Hawaii.

I'd been at BYU-Provo, in the same conference as the Hawaii Rainbow Warriors, so I knew how to handle a team on a trans-Pacific trip. For a lot of teams, it's a death trap. Players get caught up in all the leis around the neck and the swaying palm trees and the ukuleles and the hula and the macadamia nuts.

I told my team, "We're here to win basketball games. We'll have a good time later."

On our off days, we went to the Polynesian Cultural Center and Pearl Harbor. And I let them have fun too. A few players acted like knuckleheads, but I used the time as an opportunity to stress to them how important basketball and family are. I was able to get inside their hearts and minds a little more effectively because we were so far away from our everyday reality.

When we got back to Georgia, we got on a roll. We stormed through the regular season, with Terrence hitting key shots and Reggie fighting for every loose rebound. We were scrapping and hustling, and we were throwing in a little bit of that old Lakers-style show time too. We had alley-oops, dunks, passes off the backboard. We'd wheel and deal and give the crowd a thrill.

The gym was packed every night. People were yelling and screaming and painting their faces gold and black. We got some recognition from the local newspapers, and local writers wrote nice articles about us and what we were trying to accomplish. I wasn't having such a problem getting people to call into my TV show anymore.

KSU went all the way to the Peach Belt finals for the second straight year, but this time we lost by the Columbus State Cougars. After they beat us 72-56, we had to sit there and watch yet another team cut down the nets.

But in the locker room afterwards, I knew something was different. The year before, the players had packed up their belongings and gone out to the bus. Some were even laughing with each other. But not this team. They were sitting around brooding and ticked off, mad about losing. That's when I knew I had a real championship-caliber team on my hands.

Our team was down and out about the loss, but not for too long. KSU had won 24 games overall, and were in the running for an at-large bid to the NCAA Division II national tournament. We were all sitting around the computers that night, reloading the screen over and over, trying to see if we'd been invited.

And when our name came up, we all jumped up and down, hugged and high-fived. Kennesaw State was in the "little dance!"

In the first round of the 48-team NCAA Division II tournament, we played Virginia Union out of the CIAA, a traditionally African-American conference. It was a powerhouse program that had won national championships, and is famous as the alma mater of NBA star Ben Wallace.

We played so well that night, I could see the hunger in my players' eyes. We fought hard for that win, and were on to the second round. Three years earlier, I was sleeping in my office, trying to build the program from scratch. Now, Kennesaw State had won its first NCAA tournament game!

But there was no time to celebrate the watershed victory. KSU played Bowie State from Maryland the next day, and they clocked us by 25 points. They just manhandled us, and they could have beaten us by 40 if they'd really wanted to. If anything, that Bowie team showed us firsthand how serious you have to be to compete for a national title.

The locker room was dead-silent afterwards. When I walked in, I noted the clenched fists, angry expressions and heaving chests of the players as they sat there absorbing the missed opportunity. These were young men who hated to lose, and I loved each one of them for that.

I gathered the players together and addressed them as a group for the final time that season.

"Guys, are you ready for this one?" I said. "If we'd have won two more games, we'd have been off to the Elite 8. We were four games away from the national title. That's how close you are.

"But you've got to lift weights, you have to practice, and you have to improve inch by inch. We're going to get better, not bitter. If we all work together and work hard, we can bring the 2004 national championship back to Kennesaw State."

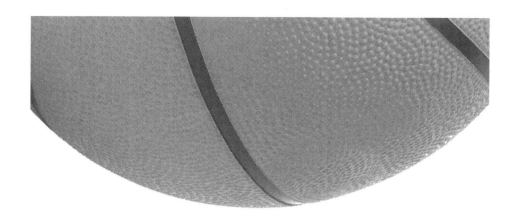

9
WINNERS TO CHAMPIONS

A T THE PEACH BELT CONFERENCE MEDIA LUNCHEON to kick off the 2003-04 season, the league's head coaches were asked to make predictions about how the PBC would stack up.

"If Kennesaw State isn't number one, y'all must be drunk," Coach Gary Toole from Augusta State said. "KSU has a chance to win a Division II national championship this year."

Once the poll was unveiled, we were picked to finish second in the league behind Columbus State, the team that had eliminated us in the championship game the previous season. I guess most of the coaches in the conference thought the script would repeat itself.

"I'm in a state of shock," I told the media after the results were announced. "We just went from national champions to second in the conference. Somewhere in there, I took a loss, and I'm trying to figure out how I got it."

We certainly didn't lose 6-5 guard Terrence Hill, the Peach Belt Conference Player of the Year from the previous season. Terrence returned as a senior.

We called Terrence "Wings" because we could isolate him out on the wing late in a ballgame and put the ball in his hands. Then we'd sit back with some hot buttery popcorn and enjoy the show.

Other teams couldn't stop Terrence. He could drive to the basket, or pull up and pop a jumper. And every time he went to the line in a crucial situation, he'd make his free throws. It was always an adventure – he'd bank or roll them in – but they'd go through the net every time.

I spoke to Terrence a week before the season began, pulling him into my office for a one-on-one meeting. I told him that if we were going to win a national championship, we didn't need him to score as much. We needed to get other players involved, I said.

"But there will probably be a time when I have to put the team on your back," I told him. "When I say, 'Wings, now's the time,' that's the signal. But I have to know right now, before the games start, that you can handle it when it gets to that time. I need to trust that you'll be ready to respond when I tap you on the shoulder."

"Yes, sir, Coach," Terrence said. "I'll be ready. You can trust me."

In one early game, a road contest at Lenoir Rhyne, we were down by two points with less than a minute remaining. Lenoir Rhyne had the ball, and I called a trap play.

Most coaches will expect a man-to-man defense in that situation. But I gambled with a trap play, putting two men on the ball handler, two protecting the basket, and one "interceptor" to steal a pass. This setup leaves one man wide open – if the open man gets the ball, you're burned like a bad grilled cheese sandwich.

Lenoir Rhyne took the ball right to the place on the floor where we wanted them to take it, but Georgy Joseph didn't rotate out to try and intercept the incoming pass. If we'd stolen the ball, we would have had a dunk and tied the game.

But Lenoir Rhyne found that open man, and scored to go up by four with 12 seconds remaining. It effectively put the game out of reach.

I called a time out to plan some late-game strategy. But I saw out of the corner of my eye that Terrence was off to the side, griping. He wasn't happy with my play-calling.

I didn't say anything at the time. The game wound down, and we lost to drop our early season record to 9-4. When we got to the hotel, I told Terrence I wanted to see him.

"Terrence," I said. "If you've got a problem, *nip it*. I saw you coming to the bench griping and moaning. I don't appreciate that. You're the captain of this team, and I want to win basketball games as much as you do. I need you not to second-guess me, brother." I showed him the tape of the play.

I asked, "Do you see how Georgy didn't come out of the hole?" "Yes, Coach, I'm sorry," Terrence said.

"Now, I want to show you something else," I said.

I pulled out the stat sheet. The referees had given Lenoir Rhyne 37 foul shots, and we only had 12.

"The odds were that they were going to call a foul on us and give them two more free throws," I told Terrence. "That was the way the game was being called. I'd rather roll the dice with a trap than put the game in the referees' hands. Do you see where I'm coming from?" Terrence bowed his head.

"Remember what I said at the beginning of the season?" I asked. "About me trusting you? You're going to have to trust me too. If we don't have mutual trust, we're not going to win that national championship."

That Lenoir Rhyne game would be the final loss of Terrence Hill's college career.

———————

Looking back, I think our early season home game against Armstrong Atlantic was the turning point of our season. During a practice the day beforehand, the players were griping and moaning and pointing fingers.

I finally had enough. I blew my whistle and interrupted the shooting drills.

"Stop it," I yelled. "I'm tired of this. We have to concentrate and focus.

I'm tired of all this pouting, griping and talking smack. *Cut it out!*" There were several minutes of relief. But then they started up again.

I had never walked out on my team, ever. In my opinion, I don't think a coach should *ever* turn his back on his players. But at the same time, I believe that a coach should never stop testing his team. If you test your team, that's when you find out what kind of team you've got.

"Y'all keep griping and moaning," I said, dropping my whistle on the floor. "You don't need me. I'm out of here."

And I walked out of the gym and back to my office.

Terrence, Reggie McKoy and Justin Thompson, who were our tricaptains that year, knocked on the door of my office.

"Can we talk to you, Coach?"

I was somber. "Have a seat, guys."

"Coach, we need you out there," Reggie said. "This is a big game tomorrow night."

"Let me tell you something," I replied. "I'll tell you the difference between you guys and me. I'm coaching to win a national championship. Y'all are playing to beat Armstrong. If you'll come together, and stop pointing fingers, we can win a national championship."

Terrence chimed in. "Coach, will you please come out and finish practice?"

"No," I replied. "I'm finished. I want you to take what I said out to the other players. You're going to beat Armstrong Atlantic. They can't beat us in our own building in front of our fans. But you're not going to win a national championship until you *START LISTENING TO ME!! IF YOU LISTEN TO ME, WE'LL WIN THE DAMN THING!!*"

Two days later, the headline in the local paper: "*Kennesaw Pounds Armstrong Atlantic, 76-51.*"

— — — — — —

I returned to the Beehive State with my Kennesaw State Fighting Owls for a game with Utah Valley State, a school that was transitioning from Division II to D-I. It was seven years since my 0-19 record at BYU, and my return to the state with a team that was coming off a D-II tournament appearance prompted a certain amount of media attention. People still remembered me, and I appreciated all the well-wishes from old friends.

I was just happy for the opportunity to meet our third grandchild. Sunshine and her husband had a new baby boy named Treyce.

The closest Utah Valley came to us was when it was 0-0. We came out ready to play that night, but we were also ready to crush the opposition. The score was 43-17 at halftime, and the final was nearly as frightening.

I don't want to print it here, lest it scare some kids.

As the season went on, our team featured a dynamic, balanced scoring attack. Georgy, our track star-turned-inside player, was getting better and better every game. Reggie McKoy was grabbing rebounds right and left, both defensive and offensive. We had big guys off the bench named Cardale Talley and Justin Thompson, who helped support a fourman inside rotation. On the outside, we had Terrence, tough-as-nails Tommy Thompson and an outstanding young guard named Rey Luque.

We found a 6-7 point guard named Kevin McDonald.

Seriously, how many Division II teams have a 6-foot-7 point guard?

We developed an inside game and an outside game. We could run on the fast break. We could handle and control any type of situation. Our defense was dynamic and fearsome, able to extend or clamp down. We had size, quickness and strength. Whatever teams threw at us, we always had the answer.

That team also included my son Israel, who was a sophomore. I'll be honest and tell you that the reason why he sat on the end of the bench was because the head coach was sleeping with his mother. But Israel worked his butt off during all four years he was able to play college basketball.

He did get some playing time occasionally. One time, we were playing Georgia College and the game was completely out of hand in our favor.

So I subbed Israel in.

Here's how the local newspaper described what happened next.

> With five minutes left in the game, Ingle drove the ball upcourt. As he crossed half-court, he completed four consecutive crossover dribbles, followed immediately by a stop-and-drop on his butt rollover move. He came up, while still dribbling the ball. The move is a knockoff of an old Nike commercial, but it was still impressive to see during a game.
>
> The crowd went crazy and gave him a standing ovation. The move earned a laugh from head coach and father Tony Ingle, but also earned him a seat on the bench for the rest of the game.
>
> Ingle commented that his son definitely takes after his mother.

— — — — — —

Kennesaw State was the first team in the history of the Peach Belt Conference to finish with a perfect 16-0 record.

How'd you like to go 15-1 in the conference and finish in second place? That's what happened to Francis Marion, a team that featured Lewis McCullough, a half-brother of Kevin Garnett. We beat the Patriots by just three points in our only regular-season meeting, and needed a 19-0 first-half run to do it. They outplayed us for the rest of the game, and we were fortunate to win.

In the early rounds of the conference playoffs, we destroyed USCAiken, then ground out a win over Clayton State. But in the championship game, we had to go head-to-head with Columbus State again. The pre-season coaches' poll turned out to be correct, we really were the best two teams in the league that year.

And just like the previous season's championship game, Columbus State had the strong upper hand. They were up by 15 points with four minutes to play.

The game was all but over, and it looked like the Cougars would be cutting down the nets at our expense again.

I called time out, and brought my team over to the bench.

"Guys," I said calmly. "We've got 'em right where we want 'em."

They looked at me as if I was crazy. Couldn't I see the scoreboard from where I was standing on the sidelines?

"I love you guys," I told them. "I'm just so proud to be your coach. You guys are such battlers, I just love each and every one of you."

"Here's what we're going to do," I continued. "I'm going to give you two minutes to cut this to nine. It's just a couple of possessions, you can do this. Then I'll call time out and we'll meet back here. Now I want y'all to do something for me. Repeat after me."

"Your want is my want. Your need is my need, and your hurt is my hurt."

They repeated each phrase back to me. "Now let's go out and win this championship," I said.

Two minutes of game action later, I called another time out.

"Look at the score," I said. "I just wanted to be out of double digits by now. But we're just down six."

With 30 seconds left in the game, we were tied and had to drive the length of the court. Thirty seconds later, Terrence Hill scored on jumper with a sixth of a second remaining on the clock. The final score was 72-70.

Kennesaw's winning streak was still alive, and we had earned a berth in the national postseason the old-fashioned way, by winning the Peach Belt Conference tournament championship. Heading into the NCAA tournament, we were 29-4 and ranked No. 6 in the nation.

— — — — — —

We earned the right to host the regional, and there was a lot of excitement in the air. Our little 1,000-seat gym, a place where KSU students once went during games for some quiet study time, was now an NCAA tournament venue. The whole area was fired up about it. There were a lot of legends and stories about our comeback win against Columbus State, and there were a lot more people who said they were there than actually were.

The intensity was palpable. Everybody wanted it, and everybody was loving it. But I put all my coaches in the apartments with the players, so that people wouldn't be knocking on the doors visiting and bothering them at all hours.

Our assistant coaches got the players into bed at the right times, woke them up at the right times, the whole nine yards. I got more complaints from the players about the coaches snoring than I got from the coaches about the players goofing off.

Our first round game was against Catawba, and we won easily by 15 points. It was our landmark 30th victory.

KSU was pitted against Columbus State the next night, a quick re-match of the Peach Belt title game. The Cougars had earned an at-large bid to the "little dance," and were placed in our region for geographic reasons. We didn't need the same kind of late-game heroics this time around, and we had them completely figured out. We won 70-55 to dispatch them from the national tournament.

In the regional final, we played Francis Marion, another familiar Peach Belt foe. The Patriots were the team that had finished 15-1 and second in the league, with only a single three-point loss against us. They had lost in the PBC playoffs before they could get another shot at us, and they were ready for revenge. Additionally, FMU was ranked one step higher in the national polls than we were, at No. 5, and had lost just three games all season.

So we came in as the underdogs.

But our team was clicking on all cylinders. We had that high-octane offense in junior college that I called "Wendy's," where we "got it to go" by rebounding, kicking out and shooting quickly. I was able to do the same thing at Kennesaw, but with better athletes.

We ran all over Francis Marion, and won the regional final by a score of 82-73. After the game, our fans and families ran onto the floor in a hot, noisy court-storming. We were all so excited.

Kennesaw State was going to the Elite Eight!

— — — — — —

The final three rounds of the national tournament were pre-scheduled to be held in Bakersfield, California. KSU was California dreaming, baby! I'm just glad nobody ever looked on a map.

When we got out to Bakersfield, the NCAA held a press conference for all eight participating head coaches.

Once it came to my portion, I quipped, "I've been telling our players all year that we were going to get here and get a little sand in their shoes and walk down the beach. Don't tell them we're two and a half hours away. And another thing... Kennesaw State isn't just happy or proud to be here. We're here to win a national championship."

They opened it up for questions. A reporter asked me, "Coach Ingle, Kennesaw State... where is that located?"

"We're in Kennesaw, Georgia, 20 minutes north of Atlanta on Interstate 75," I said. "We're just north of Marietta, if you know where that is."

There was another question. "Coach Ingle, you say you're here to win a national championship. Are you hoping to slip in the back door and surprise some teams here?"

"We're from Georgia," I replied. "We have a lot of pride down there. And I know no team from our state has ever won a national championship, I understand that. But this team is Kennesaw State. We're not going to walk in the back door. I never want my team to feel second-class, second-rate or second fiddle. We are proud of our accomplishments, and we have nothing to be ashamed of.

"We are going to come into the house, which is that arena over there," I continued. "We're going to walk in the front door. And we're going to walk out the front door with our trophy. You'll know what I'm talking about by the time this tournament's over." You could have heard a pin drop.

But privately, I've never been so nervous before a game in my life. We'd already played some big games, but our opponent in the Elite Eight round had me concerned. The Falcons had cleared 100 points in seven of their last eight games, including each of their NCAA contests. The prospect of stopping an attack like that scared me.

So I called Terrence into my hotel room. He asked, "You wanted to see me, Coach?" "Wings, now's the time," I said.

Terrence nodded. He understood exactly what I meant.

"When you walk out this door, the team's on your shoulders."

Kennesaw had a 10-2 run early on, and we led 51-35 at halftime. We were playing a team that scored over 100 points per ballgame, and *we* had 51 at the half. We were, basically, getting it to go.

In the press conference after the game, Terrence told the media, "When the ball is in my hands, I have control of the game."

When I woke up the morning of the semifinal against Humboldt State of California, it hit me. "If we win this one," I said to myself. "We're in the national championship game."

We'd be on CBS right before the Division I Final Four. Nobody in our conference had ever reached the title game, nobody in our state had ever done it.

But Humboldt presented a unique challenge. How many teams can you name with two 2,000-point scorers... at the same time?

In the history of BYU, there were only two players who scored 2,000 points in their careers: Devin Durrant and Danny Ainge. But the power forward and two-guard on this Californian squad had both amassed over 2,000 points each, and they were both out on the floor.

The game itself turned out to be anticlimactic. Our Owls weren't going to be denied, and we took the steam out of high-scoring Humboldt early on. We got out on their shooters and played incredible defense all night. We had a 16-point lead with three minutes left to play.

At that point, a referee walked by the bench. I yelled out, "Thomas! Thomas!"

He didn't say anything. The ball came back up the floor, and I tried calling out after him again. "Hey, Thomas! Yoo hoo, Thomas!" During a stoppage in play, the ref walked over to me.

"Coach Ingle," he said very seriously with his arms folded. "My name isn't Thomas."

"I know," I replied. "There ain't but one Thomas Edison, so don't you be inventing anything. We don't need any courtesy calls going against us right now. We want to be on TV Saturday morning!" We won, 81-67. We were on to the title game.

———————

On Saturday morning, I had a meeting in my hotel room with Terry Lenahan and Chris Poulos, two of my long-time friends and confidants, my wife and my son Tony. They all knew everything that I had been through to make it to the brink of a national championship, because they had been there through the darkest hours. There were very emotional moments as we prayed, remembered and laughed.

It felt so good to be able to laugh about moments that had been so bleak. I remembered what I'd written so many years ago: *"Life is short, serious and frail; learn from it, laugh at it, and live it well."*

I recalled that day I was fired at BYU, when I turned to the president and vice president and said, "If you want to win it all, give me a call." I was so grateful that Dr. Waples at Kennesaw State had made that call and given me a chance to prove myself.

I thought about that Kansas sunrise, about how close I was to making the dream of a broken player come true as a coach. I recalled sitting on that plane at the Wichita airport over two decades before, looking out at that day breaking over the fields as my knee was a mess of tangled and torn ligaments. I remembered the sting of feeling like I let down my parents and my girlfriend.

Jeanne eventually became my wife, and she was there in Bakersfield with me. I was so happy that she could share that moment. But I felt so sad that my mother hadn't lived to see the day her son would play for the national championship. I knew she was watching me from heaven.

I also thought about my son Golden, out in the field, helping spread the message of Christ. We were forbidden to contact him while he was on his mission, so that he could devote all his time and energy on his task.

I found out later that Golden had gone to his mission president that day.

"My dad's basketball team is playing for the national championship on CBS," he said. "Can I get special permission to take a couple hours off from my mission to watch the game?"

The mission president paused for a moment, and then replied in the form of a question.

"Who did you come to serve?"

So while we were playing for a national championship, Golden was somewhere in Colorado knocking on doors, sharing the message that Jesus Christ hears and answers prayers. He was out there building the kingdom of God on this earth, in the face of humiliation and rejection, telling people about a Heavenly Father who loves and cares for them. He also had an earthly father and family in Bakersfield, California.

Some people might think it's corny, and I don't know how others feel when they play for national championships, but I could feel a powerful spirit there that day, a strong presence.

During the two years Golden was on his mission, we won 60 games.

No men's basketball team in Division I or Division II won more games during that period. (Metro State won 60 as well.) We had a 26-game winning streak, the longest in all of American college or pro basketball that 2003-04 season. There was a junior college that year that went 37-1, but they lost their 18th game.

The game time for our final showdown with the University of Southern Indiana was set at 1 p.m. Eastern, slotted right before the two national semifinal games in Division I. So because of the three-hour time difference, local game time was 10 a.m. on the dot. So there was very little time to get completely lost in thought.

I had to get to the arena and get focused.

There are two games a coach should never have to get his team up for: the first game of the year, and a championship. You wait a long time for the first one, and you battle and struggle your way all year towards the other. As I gathered the team in the locker room before the game, I fought to find the right words to offer them.

"Guys," I said. "We're playing for the national championship, and we're playing for each other. This is something you'll remember for the rest of your life. I'm not worried about you playing hard and smart and together, all that stuff. I just want to make sure you have fun. Go out there and enjoy this game.

"Tell a teammate you love them," I continued. "Tell a teammate, 'Thank you for helping me get to this game.' There's not a guy in this room that got here because of themselves. You got here because you have teammates who love you. And if you're not into telling them out loud, then show them. Show them by hustling, by diving. Show them by drawing charges, by being smart and under control. Tell them you love them by hitting your jump shots and free throws, by playing the game the way it's supposed to be played.

"When your number gets called, you get on the floor and you play like a national champion. And if you do that, you *will* be a national champion when the buzzer sounds. You're going to see them raise that banner to the rafters, and they're going to bring out the ladders and a pair of scissors. A lot of people think that 'SNL' stands for Saturday Night Live, but it stands for Scissors, Nets and Ladders. We're going to climb up that ladder, each one of us, and we're going to cut down the nets. We're going to take pictures that last a lifetime."

"Lastly, just remember this: it's not about the rings, it's about the feeling of being the best. And we *are* the best. I feel sorry for anybody who has to play us today. They're in front of the *wrong team*."

The Kennesaw State Owls hit the Centennial Garden court, and just like that, we found ourselves down to Southern Indiana by a 10-2 count. The Screaming Eagles ran on us and slammed in a couple of backboardrattling dunks. Their players were showboating and high-fiving, trying to humiliate us into quick submission.

But we'd have none of that.

Then Georgy Joseph hit a 3-pointer from the top of the key to make it 10-5, and that was the match that lit the fuse. Kennesaw roared back, and once we had them down, we showed no mercy.

KSU went up by 20. With less than three minutes remaining in the game, Terrence Hill came up to me during a time out.

"Coach," he said. "I know how you are. But please, put my teammates in."

"What do you mean, Terrence?"

"We're going to win the game," he replied. "They're my teammates. They worked just as hard as I did, Coach. Please, put them in."

This was the two-time conference Player of the Year talking. He'd scored over 20 points in each of the three games in Bakersfield, and he had 26 in the national championship game on CBS. It was the greatest individual performance in school history. The pros were watching, and he could have padded his stats to get the attention of the European scouts or the D-League. Terrence could have gone for 30.

But Terrence wanted to share the glory.

And he didn't say, "Put the subs in, Coach." He didn't say, "Put the other players in, Coach." Terrence Hill *clearly* and *specifically* asked for his *teammates.*

Then I asked my assistant coaches for advice. They waved their hands from side to side. "No, no," they said. "This is the national championship. We can't leave anything to chance."

I don't like to go against the judgment of my assistant coaches, but this was one time when I overruled them.

I'd watched No. 24 run up and down the floor for the last time. I went over to the bench, and I did what Terrence asked me to do.

I put his teammates in.

Most title games are very close, and it's very rare for players on the end of the bench to make it into a game during which everything's on the line. One of the players I subbed in was my own son Israel, who'd sat down by the water bucket all season.

But Israel scored three points in that game. That little boy that I'd whipped because he wouldn't tell me why he was suspended from school, who stood up for his daddy, was on the floor when the final buzzer sounded and the scoreboard flashed: *Kennesaw State 84, Southern Indiana 59.*

There was a shot at the buzzer that we missed, which would have given us the widest margin of victory in any NCAA championship game. Most national title games are decided by single digits.

I don't care what anybody says, I know the Lord was on our side that day.

Israel wore Golden's jersey that season: number 43. I asked Golden once why he picked that number.

"It stands for 'Love Mom,'" he said. "Four, three."

(I was just glad it didn't mean "Hate Dad.")

Before every game I coach, I turn to Jeanne and hold up fingers during introductions. One, four, three. "I love you."

If she's not there, I pick out an empty seat. If I don't do that, I get nervous during the game that she's not there in spirit. So I never forget.

Later on that summer, when we ordered national championship rings, everybody in my family got one – including Jeanne, who never gave up on me. My daughter Sunshine received one as well, she was always writing the team letters, wishing us luck and offering congratulations when we won a big game. Tony got one too, he was our team manager. Eliott, my oldest, got a ring; he was always coming to games, cheering his lungs out for his brothers. So did Golden, our little missionary!

When that game was over, I ran out on the floor and embraced Israel. There are highlight tapes of that game that show my son and I crying and hugging. I gave all my players hugs. I hugged people I'd never met before in my life. I think I might have hugged some Southern Indiana guys in all the confusion. There were people running around everywhere, and confetti all over the place.

Our team gathered around center court, holding and touching the NCAA Division II national championship trophy. We took a team picture together, and we were interviewed on CBS. It was all one big, happy blur.

We were national champions, we'd won it all. We were the best.

— — — — — —

Ray Harper from Kentucky Wesleyan, seven-time Division II Coach of the Year and two-time national champion, called me to congratulate me after we won. "Hey Tony," he said. "You won the national championship, so that means you're going to win national Coach of the Year. That's just the way it always seems to work, you know. Better take your suit to the dry cleaners... but you wear it to about every game anyway, don't you?"

At the NABC awards banquet in San Antonio, my name was called as the recipient of the 2004 NCAA Division II Coach of the Year award. From the podium, I could imagine Golden out there in the audience with light in his eyes. He was right where we'd been sitting together in 1997 when he told me I'd make it to that stage someday.

I got very emotional, and it was a serene moment.

"I know that I won this award for what my team did, and I know this has more to do with them, my family and the Lord than with me," I said as I held the plaque in my hands. "There have been a lot of coaches who've won this award before, and there will be a lot of coaches who will win this after me. But nobody's been any more honored and proud to receive it than I am.

"Seven years ago, I sat out there in that audience, unemployed. I'm the same person today that I was then. I went 0-19, and I couldn't win a ballgame. I stood up for my team, I coached my team, I did the best I could. Now I'm standing here with this award that you've been so kind to bestow upon me. I accept this award on behalf of all those who believed in me, believed in our program, and who love the game of basketball."

Jeanne and I go to the Final Four every year, and one of my sons always tags along with us. Golden came off his mission in the fall of 2004, so in 2005 it was automatically his turn in the rotation.

We were all sitting there in the stands as the tens of thousands of fans poured into the Edward Jones Dome in St. Louis.

Golden suddenly said, "Daddy, daddy, look!"

He pointed up to the Jumbotron, and there was a trivia question on the screen. It read:

What school won the 2004 NCAA Division II men's basketball championship?

A few seconds later, in bright white letters five stories high, came the answer:

Kennesaw State (Ga.)

EPILOGUE

D
URING THE SUMMER AND FALL OF 2004, THERE WAS A lot of talk in the air about Kennesaw State moving to Division I. There are certain criteria that an institution has to meet in order to start the process, and schools are required to give notice to the NCAA before December 1 in order to begin the transition the following year.

Eight months after we won the national championship, school president Betty Siegel and athletic director Dr. Dave Waples announced KSU's intention to move up to the NCAA's top flight. The Owls would begin a four-year reclassification period in 2005-06, and join the Atlantic Sun Conference.

We'd done everything we could do at the Division II level, and it was always my dream to chase a Division I championship. So I saw the transition as inevitable. But because of my time at Brigham Young, I knew what we were getting into. At the same time, I knew the difference between a well-established D-I program and a school just beginning to find its way.

Kennesaw State had one final season at the D-II level before starting the reclassification period. I wanted to make sure that we finished strong, and that we followed up our national title with a repeat trip to the NCAA tournament. And even though we'd made it look easy the previous two years, it's hard to get into the national postseason.

It's harder than pulling the hair out of my mother-in-law's homemade biscuits.

We had the target on our backs that any national champion has to wear, and we were ranked No. 2 in the nation coming into the 2004-05 season. Every time we played, opponents would get fired up and work extra-hard to take down the champs. It's difficult to match that intensity and excitement night in and night out.

To us, each game was just that – another game.

But we weathered the storm with the players we had. We lost Terrence Hill, two-time Peach Belt Player of the Year and first-team Division II All-American, to graduation. We also lost Reggie McKoy, who had more total rebounds (363) than anyone else in the country during our championship year. We had a team that year that was expected to do everything, was given nothing, and ended up accomplishing a lot.

Exciting changes were all around us, but we had to stay focused. Kennesaw State was building a beautiful new Convocation Center that we'd move into at the start of the 2005-06 school year, and our final D-II season would also be our last in the old 1,000-seat Spec Landrum Center. But during the spring, workers were tearing the walls out to build a new weight room, so we weren't able to practice there. We had to go to local high school gyms to get our drills in.

We ended up back in the NCAA tournament, where we lost in the first round. We were taken out by our old Peach Belt rivals Columbus State, by five points in overtime. I guess they got the last laugh on us. But we finished 24-6, and in so doing became the first team in league history to achieve four consecutive 20-win seasons. Over our last three years in Division II, we won 84 games, averaging 28 victories per season.

In 2005-06, we played our first full Division I schedule. We also had to operate under a completely new set of rules; for instance, some players who were D-II eligible didn't meet the academic requirements for D-I.

Our cupboard was bare, and that wasn't a condition limited to the roster. Stace Tedford, Jeff Jones and Greg Matta all left my bench to accept head coaching jobs at other institutions, rewards for their great success at Kennesaw. I was happy and proud for them, but we were starting over from scratch again. If it wasn't for Gary Dyksterhouse, a volunteer coach who helped me through the summer months, our first transition year would have been a complete disaster.

We put together the best team we could under the circumstances, and I didn't expect to win more than three or four games. Teams that go through reclassification to D-I often go through a period of extreme culture shock.

As he had done four years earlier, Golden returned to Kennesaw State to help his daddy build a new program's foundation. He was our starting point guard that season, and I cherished the opportunity to watch him run up and down the floor in that No. 43 jersey, a tribute to his mother. "Love Mom."

We were very, very small to say the least. Our primary post threat was 6-3 Andre Morgan, and we did have one 6-7 inside guy named Ryan Nelson. The only problem was that he weighed 169 pounds.

But we competed every night to the best of our combined abilities.

In early November, we started the 2005-06 season in Fairbanks, Alaska at the Top of the World Classic. Our first D-I game came against the University of Denver, the preseason pick to win the Sun Belt Conference. They had a 6-11 kid named Yemi Nicholson who ate us up in the post. We lost by 12 points.

In the next night's game, I came face to face with an old adversary from my BYU days. Billy Tubbs was the head coach of Lamar University by then, a Southland Conference school in Texas. As he always had, he recruited a lineup full of big, long-armed athletes who loved to play full-court pressure defense. Much like the time his TCU squad crushed my 0-19 Cougars by 41 points, we were simply outmanned.

We tried to match their explosiveness with a strategy I like to call "na-na-na-boo-boo." We played keep-away until we got an open shot. We were just trying to stay as close as we could for as long as we could.

Our team didn't have much depth, so I subbed in Israel. He ended up having 10 points in that game. Three of those points came after an incredible bullet pass from Golden; little 5-foot-10 Israel had two gigantic Lamar players draped all over him, but somehow got the ball to the basket. Then he made the and-one with the foul shot.

With three minutes to play, we had Billy Tubbs' team down by 30 points. And we had him angry and frustrated, yelling at his players. At one point, the officials gave him a technical foul for arguing calls.

We got back to the hotel after the game, and we had a big family hug. Golden and Israel were part of that team. Tony was an assistant coach, and Jeanne flew out to support us. I was so glad that my family was there when I got that win.

It had taken me 21 tries, but I finally had my first victory as a Division I head coach.

— — — — — —

Our reclassification period is now complete. Kennesaw State will become a fully fledged Division I member in the 2009-10 season. After that four-year wait, we will finally be eligible for the Atlantic Sun Conference tournament and the national postseason. We're standing at the threshold, knocking at the door, ready to step into a new world.

The transition period was a very tough time for all of us, especially for those in the administration. They've had to budget more money to ensure that our athletic department can operate at Division I standards. A main reason why the NCAA doesn't grant full membership right away is that there are always growing pains associated with reclassification. Those four years gave us the opportunity to become accustomed to the increased financial, academic and infrastructure burdens that D-I schools face.

KSU won't enter the top flight with the same financial advantages that the Dukes, Carolinas and UCLA's of the world enjoy. But as Coach Wooden once told me, "Don't let what you don't have interfere what you can do."

Instead of focusing on the difficulties, instead of making excuses and cursing my fate, I choose to look at this transition as a great opportunity. It's been a chance for us to build a university-wide work ethic that will benefit us well into the future. We've all worked very hard.

I've used this time to make sure that our men's basketball program has a strong foundation for the future, but it's been a long process. Have you ever driven by a construction site day after day, and thought, "Are they ever going to get anything built?" Maybe you've had the experience of coming back from a week's vacation, and there's a new restaurant there with a "Grand Opening" sign. Maybe it's even a Wendy's, and there's a line of cars in the drive-thru, all getting it to go.

I consider myself to be in the construction industry too, in a metaphorical sense. I'm in the dream-building business. I tell my players, "You bring your shoes, you bring your jersey, and you bring your dream to the court."

I believe that dreams can come true, because mine did.

My dream was to win a national championship. It took 31 years, faith, patience, love and support to see it come to fruition. For the family and friends who helped me along the way, it became their dream too.

I have a new dream now. I want to get to the top of the mountain again, this time as a Division I head coach. I want to win it all.

I'm prepared to face this new challenge head on, to build another program at the same school. We have a strong and solid foundation that's taken four years to dig and fill, and we're now ready to build the castle of our dreams on top of it. I am bringing everything I have into this battle, everything in my memory bank, my briefcase, everything in my heart, mind and soul.

And I wouldn't bet against me.

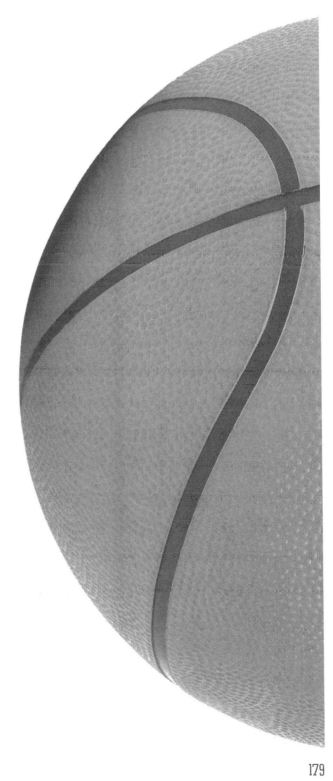

APPENDIX

COACHING ACCOMPLISHMENTS

National Champions (NCAA Division II) 2004

National Coach of the Year, NABC (NCAA Division II) 2004

National Coach of the Year, Molten (NCAA Division II) 2004

South Atlantic Region Champions [36 teams] (NCAA Division II) 2004

Peach Belt Conference Regular Season Champions (NCAA Division II) 2004

Peach Belt Tournament Champions (NCAA Division II) 2004

All-Time winningest head coach at Kennesaw State University Peach Belt Conference Regular Season Champions (NCAA Division II) 2003

Naismith Awards and Atlanta Tip Off Club State College Coach of the Year (NCAA Division II) 2004

Peach Belt Conference Coach of the Year (NCAA Division II) 2003

Atlanta Tip Off Club Junior College Coach of the Year (NCAA Division II) 1988

Atlanta Journal-Constitution AAAA HS Coach of the Year 1982

Inducted, Cherokee County Sports Hall of Fame (NCAA Division II) 2009

OTHER EXPERIENCES

26-game winning streak (longest in all of basketball in 2004)

Scouted for Utah Jazz (NBA)

Founder and Executive Director, John & Nellie Wooden Awards (five years)

Coached in eight NCAA Tournaments (five D-I, three D-II)

Coached in two NIT tournaments (one postseason, one preseason)

Color analyst for KSL-TV/SportsWest for Mountain West Conference
  Host, "Courtside with Tony Ingle" (airs in 12 states, available in 7
  million homes)
Coached two NBA players (Shawn Bradley and Andy Toolson)
Board member, Atlanta Tip Off Club
Producer of DVD instructional video, "Dribbling to Dreams"
Stand-up comedy, Johnny B's Comedy Club (Provo, Utah)
Director
Member, National Speakers Association

EDUCATION

North Georgia College, Master's Degree in Education
Huntingdon College, Bachelor of Arts in Physical Education

FAMILY

Married 35 years to Jeanne - five children, five grandchildren
Ingle family was nationally known as the "Little Nuggets;" ranked among best
  NBA halftime shows in the 1980's and performed on TBS, NBC and CBS

SPEAKING TESTIMONIALS

"Tony is a highly effective speaker; he is very real and authentic."

Dr. Stephen R. Covey, author/speaker

"We heard sales people quoting Tony months after he gave his speech."

Kyrus Frames, RBM Atlanta Mercedes Benz

"Tony was our keynote speaker at our international convention and
he had us laughing and crying at the same time."

**Dave Riley, CEO Pro Image CorpFor speaking engagements and
other products:**

www.tonyingle.com

CONTACT INFORMATION

We welcome any comments you might have in regards to the book and what benefit you received from the Coach Tony Ingle Story by e-mailing us at

COACH@TONYINGLE.COM

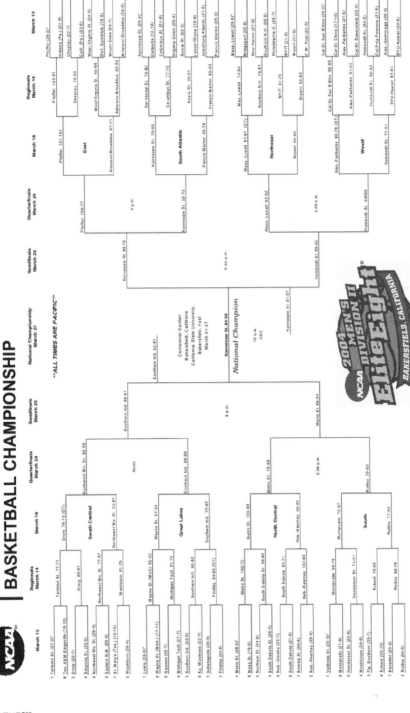

2004 NCAA Division II Men's
BASKETBALL CHAMPIONSHIP

"ALL TIMES ARE PACIFIC"

Centennial Garden
Bakersfield, California
California State University,
Bakersfield, host
March 24–27

National Champion

10 a.m.
CBS

2004 MEN'S DIVISION II EliteEight
BAKERSFIELD, CALIFORNIA

ACKNOWLEDGEMENTS

TONY INGLE

Obviously, there are so many people to thank, but I do want to express sincere appreciation to all my coaches that helped me develop as a person and player: Brady Creel, Gary Cochran, Leonard Whaley, Melvin Ottinger, Dick Coleman, Neal Posey.

I'd also like to thank my great assistant coaches through the years: Mike Wade, Ron Wheeler, Ron Smith, Gary Peters, Jeff Jones, Stace Tedford, Greg Matta, Gary Dyksterhouse, Montez Robinson, Che Roth, Evan Black and Tony Ingle, Jr, Russ Zaugg and Greg Kite.

Head coaches who hired and mentored me were Roger Reid, Steve Jones and Mike Anderson. Thanks also to athletic director Pete Adams, and assistant coaching colleagues Charles Bradley and Jeff Reinhart.

Others that have helped me especially through the tough times: Stephen Zimmerman, Dave Hagan, Dave Riley, Chris Poulos, Sam Swain, Keith and Lynn Whitworth, Mike Jacobson, Gregg Hayes, John and Jason Hewlett, Glen Tuckett, Lavell Edwards, Frank Layden, David Miles, Stephen Covey, Dale Murphy and my dearest of friends Terry and Georgia Lenahan.

Thanks to Bobby Cremins, Bob Reinert, Jackie Bradford for great advice, and a special thank you to Dr. Dave Waples for hiring me at Kennesaw State. Thanks also to Dr. Waples' hiring committee for their faith in me: Scott Whitlock, Mike Sansing, Jerome Ratchford, Mike Redd and Colby Tilley.

And finally, a special thanks to the Dalton Gang: Tim Jones, Lane Newberry, John Oxford, Steve Henderson, Lamar McClure, Mike Douglas, Mike Foster, Alan Wells, Jack Crump, Richard and Tom Phillips. Thanks also to Shirley Whitworth, and my dear sisters Bev, Kay, Donna,

Sheila and Cindy... and especially our president Dr. Betty Siegel for her continued support.

KYLE WHELLISTON

IT ALL BEGAN ONE JANUARY AFTERNOON IN 2006, WHEN ESPN.com sent me to an Atlanta suburb to write a story about a new Division I team called Kennesaw State. The Owls were improbably leading the Atlantic Sun conference with an 9-1 record halfway through the regular season. I showed up at the Convocation Center during the team practice, hoping for a chance to get some quotes from the coach afterwards. Mistaking me for a spy for the opposing team, Tony Ingle kicked me out of the gym within ten seconds of my arrival.

There were no hard feelings, though. After the game, Coach Ingle spent over five hours regaling me with tales in his office. I laughed until my jaw became dislodged from its socket. But I was also struck by his true and genuine nature, how honest and real his story of struggle and determination is. To this day, no other head coach has ever made me cry during an interview. Never, ever let this guy around Barbara Walters!

Coach and I lost touch for a few years – college basketball is a busy world – but I ran into him again at the 2009 Atlantic Sun conference tourney. His KSU team was in its final season reclassifying from Division II to D-I and wasn't yet eligible for the postseason, but he was there watching games with his son Tony, Jr. anyway. It was late at night, after a quarterfinal doubleheader, and I called out to him. He told me that no other article ever written about him had ever captured his essence quite like mine did, and it was one of the kindest compliments I've ever received.

Then he asked me to co-write the book he'd been trying so hard to write for the previous four years. It took me less time to say "yes" than it took Coach Ingle to kick me out of the Kennesaw State Convocation Center.

I want to thank my proofreader Robert Workman, my designer Roni Lagin, and my father. Also, thanks to all my friends at The Mid-Majority for their generosity and support these past five years. Thanks to my editors from my ESPN.com days and to my boss at Basketball Times, John Akers. Special thanks to Jeanne, Golden and Tony, Jr. for opening your home to me and showing me so much love and kindness. But most of all, thanks to Coach Ingle for the opportunity, for which I'm very honored. This book would not have been possible without suspended gravity, Kaliber, the Acworth Starbucks, or all the hoses and sprinkers and fire trucks in Cobb County. You can't stop the Mormon Magnet.

53603531R00112

Made in the USA
Columbia, SC
21 March 2019